Dogsteps — A New Look

A better understanding of dog gait through cineradiography (moving x-rays)

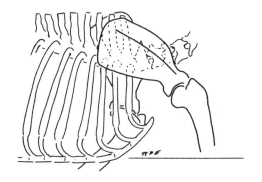

Cineradiography — What is it?

At Harvard University's Museum of Comparative Zoology, a specially-equipped laboratory makes possible the simultaneous photographing and fluoroscoping of dogs as they move at controlled speeds on a treadmill. This procedure, known as cineradiography, is similar to "moving X-rays." To make the films more graphic for the layman, Mrs. Elliott has traced them in simple drawings that enable us to clearly see what happens "inside" at the corresponding stage of the dog's movement.

DOGSTEPS — A New Look

A better understanding of dog gait through cineradiography ("moving X-rays")

by RACHEL PAGE ELLIOTT

Illustrations, motion sequences and diagrams by the author.
Additional drawings by Eve Andrade, Marcia Schlehr and Chris Lewis Brown.

THIRD EDITION

Third Printing

DORAL PUBLISHING

Published by Doral Publishing, Sun City, Arizona
Printed in the United States of America.

ISBN: 0-944875-73-4
Library of Congress Number: 00-105573

Cover & interior design by The Printed Page, using CorelDraw® and Corel Ventura™ 8

Publisher's Cataloging-in-Publication
(Provided by Quality Books, Inc.)

Elliott, Rachel Page.
    Dogsteps : a new look / by Rachel Page Elliott ;
    [edited by] Lisa Liddy ; illustrations by the author, Eve Andrade,
Chris Lewis Brown, Marcia Schlehr. -- 3rd ed.
    p. cm.
    Includes bibliographical references and index.
    LCCN: 00-105573
    ISBN: 0-944875-73-4

    1. Dogs--Anatomy. 2. Gait in animals. 3. Dogs--
Breeding.   I. Liddy, Lisa. II. Title.

SF767.D6E38 2000   636.7'089276
                        QBI00-699

To my husband,
whose patience made it possible.

RACHEL PAGE ELLIOTT has long been one of America's most respected authorities on dog gait. Her unique illustrated lectures on the subject have been hailed by audiences all over the world—throughout the United States (including Hawaii and Alaska), Canada, England, Scotland, Wales, the Scandinavian countries, Europe and Australia—and have done much to awaken breeders to the importance of recognizing the rights and wrongs in the ways dogs move.

When *Dogsteps* (largely based upon the lectures) was published in 1973, the Dog Writers Association of America acclaimed it "Best Dog Book of the Year" and it continues to be the eminent book on dog gait.

Mrs. Elliott's dedication to the pursuit of knowledge is never-ending. Her continuing studies with cineradiography equipment at Harvard University's Museum of Comparative Zoology have provided fresh insights on bone and joint motion, which she presents in this important new edition.

Pagey Elliott was born in 1913 in Lexington, Massachusetts, the youngest of a large family who shared their lives with horses, dogs and other animals. She is a graduate of Radcliffe College, now Harvard University. She continues to make her home at River Road Farm along the Concord River in Carlisle, Massachusetts, where she and her late husband, Mark, raised their three children. They and their four grandchildren have always participated in a variety of outdoor sports.

Over the years, the Elliotts have owned many breeds, but main attention has been on Golden Retrievers. The Foundation of their Featherquest Kennel was Goldwood Toby, trained and handled by Pagey, and the first Golden to earn a Utility Degree (UD) in obedience. Toby's son, Tennessee's Jack Daniels, also owner-handled, was the first New England raised retriever to win a qualifying stake in licensed retriever trials. The Featherquest honor roll includes many show champions.

Mrs. Elliott is a past president of the Golden Retriever club of America and of the Ladies' Dog Club of Massachusetts. She served many years on the board of the OFA (Orthopedic Foundation for Animals) and has twice been named "Dogdom's Woman of the Year." In 1998, the American Kennel Club honored her as the first recipient of their Lifetime Achievement award in the field of conformation.

In addition to her ongoing canine interests, Pagey continues to write, cut wooden jigsaw puzzles, raise Connemara ponies, and compete with one of her Golden Retrievers in the sport of agility.

Contents

Foreword

There has long been need for understandable information on various points of great concern to dog breeders.

Too often, people supervise the breeding of dogs without knowledge of what they are doing to the breed from a hereditary standpoint. Of the many faults that can be produced, probably the most obvious are those which contribute to lameness or poor gait.

Mrs. Elliott has recognized this need for the education of dog breeders in the basics of sound gait and performance. Based upon her years of association with show and field trial dogs, study of reel after reel of movie film, and the application of her findings to her own dogs, she has prepared this fine book.

It is especially aimed for the layman, with clear, simple wording and easy-to-understand drawings. Study of this material will aid in recognizing what is good and what is faulty action, and the application of what is learned should produce rewarding results for the conscientious dog breeder.

I compliment Mrs. Elliott for her deep insight into problems, her tireless work, and her devotion to the improvement of dog breeds by careful selection of parents. I hope this high quality book will be the first of a series clearly showing what can be achieved by proper breeding of dogs.

—E.W. Tucker, D.V.M.

(Past president of the American Veterinary Medical Association, and of the Massachusetts Veterinary Association.)

One of the most valuable and pleasurable experiences of my life has been my long association and cherished friendship with Rachel Page Elliott. I was fortunate enough to have had the opportunity to travel with Pagey, primarily during the 1970's and '80's, accompanying her to numerous seminars throughout the country. My job was to give a presentation on canine anatomy as a preliminary basis for her inspirational film and lecture on canine movement, and how a dog's gait is correlated with his structure and soundness.

I had the good fortune to spend many hours of discussion and deliberation with her on this subject during these trips, as well as the opportunity to come to know the remarkable person that she is. Pagey has always been an inquisitive, persistent and tireless worker in her pursuit of information. She has also been truly dedicated to her desire to help the dog enthusiast, whether he be novice or long time exhibitor, breeder or judge, to better understand the fundamentals of sound movement. I personally learned a great deal through my association with Pagey, and I consider her my highly respected and valued mentor, not only for her expertise in this field, but also as a most knowledgeable and devoted authority on her beloved Golden Retrievers.

Based upon her lectures came the publication of the first edition of her book *Dogsteps* in 1973. This reference work was a much needed and well-received addition to authoritative canine literature. Since then, she pursued her research with diligent and painstaking work utilizing cineradiography with Dr. Farish Jenkins at Harvard University's Museum of Comparative Zoology. In 1983, she shared these radiographic findings on canine bone and joint motion with the dog fraternity in the second edition, entitled *The New Dogsteps*.

These new findings were received with controversy from some individuals, but as a veterinarian with great interest in canine anatomy and movement, I am thoroughly convinced that there should be no contention over facts she so clearly presented.

It is with great anticipation that we have been looking forward to this latest revision of Mrs. Elliott's authoritative book, if indeed there can be further additions or improvements over the previous version. This valuable work needs to be studied thoughtfully and thoroughly, if we are to fully understand and appreciate good canine movement.

—Elizabeth Trainor, D.V.M.

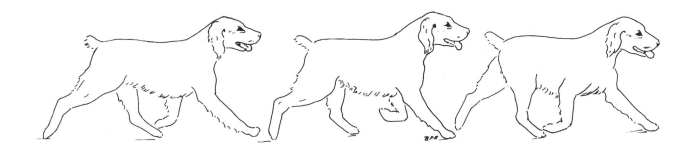

A strong, even gait is desirable in all breeds…

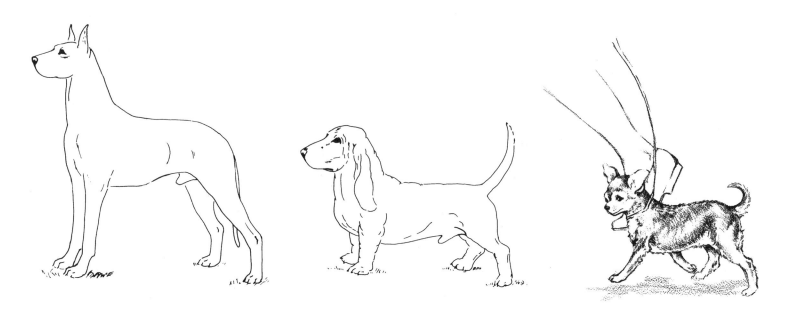

no matter the size…   *the shape…*   *or purpose.*

Author's Introduction

Dogsteps—*A New Look* is designed to make easier the recognition of normal and faulty ways in which the dog moves.

Gait tells much about a dog's structure that is not revealed when he is standing still, as it reflects his physical coordination, balance of body and soundness. The correlation between gait and structure is frequently misunderstood and—in a time when growing interest in dogs as family pets tends to lessen awareness of the need for stamina and working ability—its significance is often overlooked.

Sound movement contributes to the health and normal lifespan of all dogs. It is as desirable a feature in the family pet as it is important to the usefulness of dogs for hunting, farm work, police duty or racing; and without it show winners can never achieve true excellence. Also, sound dogs are happier dogs. This emphasis is not to detract from the value of type and temperament, which are necessary for the preservation of any breed, but rather to underline the truth of the old saying, *"As a dog moves, so is he built."*

Dogs do not all move alike. Differences in size and shape influence their way of going. The flashy step of a small terrier, for example, or the brisk trot of a Welsh Corgi, is not the same as the easy, loose stride of Bloodhounds or Newfoundlands. And the spirited drive of proud-headed Setters lends contrast to the patient scent- trailing action of Basset Hounds. Through the centuries man has developed various kinds of dogs to meet his needs and his fancies, and their individuality today is the result of long years of selective breeding.

Varied as dogs are, however, the principle by which they cover the ground is the same for all and is dictated by nature. This is the law of balance and gravity, which is constantly directed toward efficient forward motion with a minimum waste of effort—the key to good movement. When man upsets this law through inattention to sound structure, nature has to compensate for his mistakes with counter-balances which show up in faulty gaiting patterns.

Incorrect movement, either temporary or permanent, can also occur as a result of lameness due to sprains, breaks, cuts, bruises or other reasons, but these should be recognized for what they are and not confused with inherited defects. Faults vary in severity and frequency from dog to dog and from breed to breed, but they are universal to the canine world—constantly challenging our search for perfection.

While one does not have to be a student of anatomy to appreciate dogs, the ability to recognize good and poor movement is basic for a working knowledge. To be sure, movement is quicker than the eye, but the educated eye knows better what to look for, and the eye that understands is not easily deceived. In the course of my study on this subject, I have taken slow-motion movies, from which I have drawn animated sequences showing various phases of leg action at different angles to the viewer. Included also, are a few skeletal suggestions to help the reader visualize bone and joint movement beneath coat and muscles. Some of the illustrations may appear to be exaggerated— actually they are not; most are tracings from frames of my movie films.

There is no intention to associate any of the technical sketches with a particular breed—for all are vulnerable. Except for some of the pencil drawings showing dogs at work, most of the studies portray dogs moving at the trot, as this gait is generally considered best for evaluating movement as it relates to build. However, some examples of other gaits have also been included for identification and comparison.

For newcomers, interest in *Dogsteps—A New Look* may be simply in owning a good dog. Nevertheless, we hope there is something of value here for **all** dog fanciers, and particularly the many breeders who are striving to raise better puppies.

Addendum

Life is a constant process of learning that brings deeper understanding. Since the initial publication of this book in 1973, I have been privileged to study canine bone and joint motion at Harvard University's Museum of Comparative Zoology where there is a specially equipped laboratory for simultaneously photographing and fluoroscoping animals as they move at controlled speeds on a treadmill. This procedure is known as cineradiography, like moving X-rays.

My investigation was at first oriented toward the study of hip dysplasia. Not surprisingly, this led to other aspects of dog structure and answered numerous questions that have long puzzled me, particularly in regard to the dog's front assembly, how it really functions, and why a 45 degree angle of the shoulder blade is only a myth—in contradiction to the many writings that describe such an angle as essential to ideal conformation. The findings were further substantiated by lateral view X-rays of dogs in standing position. What we have failed to recognize is the mobility of the shoulder blade as it lifts and swings in coordination with the upper arm, together with the crucial influence of shape of the ribcage and the muscular forces of both. Cineradiography also shows beyond a doubt why dogs normally reach toward the center line of travel rather than moving with the legs parallel.

It is with a feeling of responsibility that I share the radiographic findings with fellow dog fanciers, for I realize how ideas that upset or challenge long standing theories or concepts can create controversy. I do not aim to persuade—I offer the new material in this edition only to present and discuss the findings as they have been revealed to me.

Rachel Page Elliott

Rachel Page Elliott

Acknowledgments

Much appreciation is extended to the many friends who contributed their time in making their dogs available for filming and for the fluoroscopic study of bone and joint motion illustrated in the pages of this book—a study that has opened our eyes to the reality of the working skeleton. This research would not have been possible without the cooperation of Harvard University's Museum of Comparative Zoology where I was allowed access to special laboratory facilities, particularly through the kindness of Dr. Farish Jenkins, Professor of Biology and Curator of Vertebrate Paleontology at the Museum. Dr. Jenkins' help, together with a generous grant from the Orthopedic Foundation for Animals, made this study possible. A silent partner through the entire project was Dr. Edgar Tucker of the Concord Animal Hospital, whose dedication to educating dog owners as to the importance of good structure and stable temperament was a constant source of inspiration. Dr. Peter Morey of the Carlisle Animal Hospital also contributed to the project through his cooperation in taking standing X-rays of dogs.

My sister, Priscilla Rose, gave valuable suggestions, not the least of which was the original title "Dogsteps." Artists Margaret Estey and my son-in-law Maris Platais offered wise counsel on diagrammatic illustrations. Thanks, too, to Eve Andrade whose beautiful pencil drawings of dogs at work brought life to the text.

For this third edition Marcia Schlehr has shared her talent and extensive knowledge of anatomy and gait, and I am grateful for her help with editing and some of the illustrations. Dr. Elizabeth Trainor gave generously with her time and constructive advice, and my close friend and overseas travel companion, Kathy Liebler, carefully reviewed each page of the manuscript. Credit also goes to my son Mark David Elliott, Jr., who, so like his father, was always ready to help clarify parts of the text. I must mention, too, our faithful housekeeper, Alberta White, who freed endless hours for my work.

I will always remember the encouragement given me by Ellsworth Howell, founder of Howell Book House, not only in pursuing my idea for the first publication of *Dogsteps*, 1973, but also the second edition, entitled *The New Dogsteps,* 1983. Dr. Alvin Grossman of Doral Publishing Company has now taken El's place, with confidence and willingness to go ahead with a third updated printing that continues the timeless message of the need for sound structure and careful breeding programs. My appreciation runs deep.

Rachel Page Elliott

Rachel Page Elliott

Chapter 1

The Language of Dog Anatomy and Comparative Skeletons

Terms Commonly Used in Describing the Dog's Outer Appearance

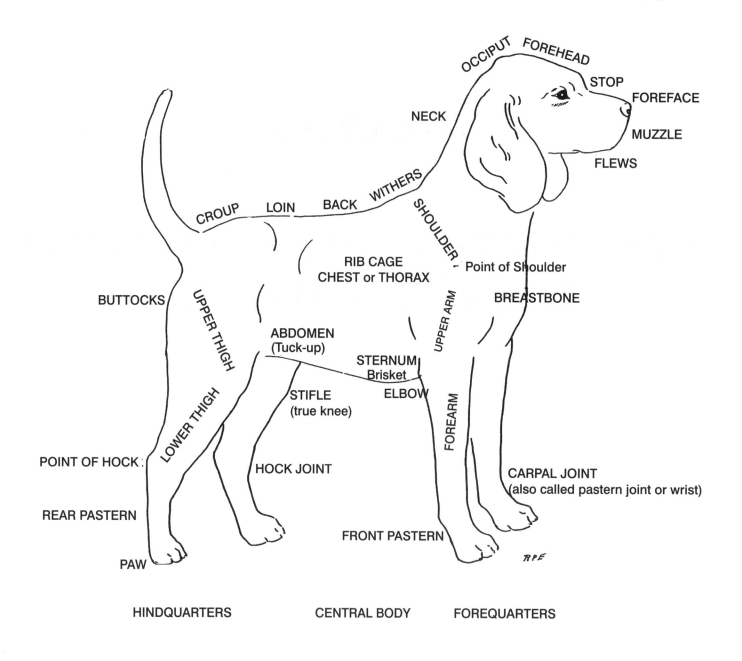

OCCIPUT FOREHEAD
STOP
FOREFACE
NECK
MUZZLE
FLEWS
WITHERS
CROUP LOIN BACK
SHOULDER
RIB CAGE
CHEST or THORAX
Point of Shoulder
BUTTOCKS
UPPER THIGH
UPPER ARM
BREASTBONE
ABDOMEN
(Tuck-up)
STERNUM
Brisket
ELBOW
LOWER THIGH
STIFLE
(true knee)
FOREARM
POINT OF HOCK
HOCK JOINT
CARPAL JOINT
(also called pastern joint or wrist)
REAR PASTERN
FRONT PASTERN
PAW
RPE

HINDQUARTERS   CENTRAL BODY   FOREQUARTERS

Terms Must Be Understood To Be Meaningful

To make certain that we are all speaking the same language in the pages that follow, skeletal diagrams of the dog, the horse and man are included here. All three of these species share the same scientific nomenclature, but much of the common language used around dogs comes from the paddock. A few words have become misconstrued or ambiguous due to the present gap between dog and horse followers, or through translation from other languages, but most of the parlance remains intact.

In spite of their structural differences—and there are important ones—horses and dogs share much in common, and the principles applying to sound conformation and gait are applicable to both. Both vary in breed type according to purpose, both come in various shapes and sizes, and both exhibit gaiting characteristics that are influenced by the differences. Describing the horse and the dog are such expressions as *body balance, smooth or choppy action, steep or sloping shoulders, long or short coupled, well ribbed up, straight of hock or stifle, cowhocks, twisting or sickle hocks, weak or strong pasterns, flipping, pounding, paddling, winging, overreaching,* etc. With what other animal is the dog compared so compatibly?

Even so, there are some dog fanciers who talk of their dogs in terms applicable to man—perhaps because of the lack of opportunity for first hand acquaintance with horses. For example, the carpal joint is referred to as the wrist, the stifle joint as the knee, or the hock as the heel; and because the dog is actually a toe-walker, the entire area from hock to paw is spoken of as the foot. The word "hock" is one of the most seriously misconstrued words in the canine language because it is often confused with the rear pastern. Breed standards, in describing conformation, usually call for good or moderate bend of hock. This is a justified qualification, but the unwary newcomer can be easily misled if someone tells him his dog should stand "straight in the hock" (for show purposes), when the reference is actually to the rear pastern.

The double meaning and interchange of terms can be perplexing, but fortunately the confusion is something we can get accustomed to as we gain understanding and confidence. Perhaps of more serious concern are the misleading and conflicting references relating to the way dogs should or should not move. Mindful of this, readers are urged to look into the works on anatomy and locomotion listed on page 125. In spite of their differing opinions, they are a worthwhile addition to a dog owner's library.

Comparative Anatomical Diagrams

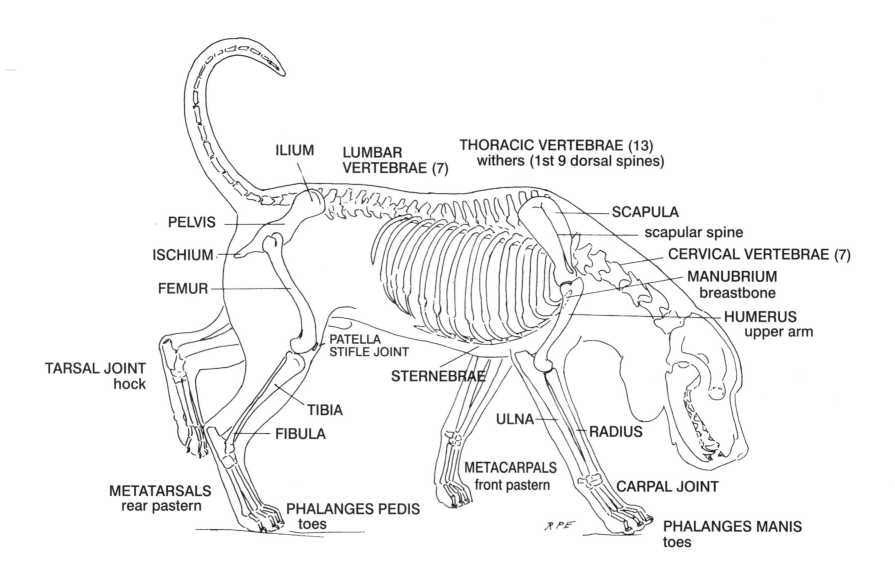

ILIUM

LUMBAR VERTEBRAE (7)

THORACIC VERTEBRAE (13)
withers (1st 9 dorsal spines)

PELVIS

SCAPULA

scapular spine

ISCHIUM

CERVICAL VERTEBRAE (7)

FEMUR

MANUBRIUM
breastbone

HUMERUS
upper arm

PATELLA
STIFLE JOINT

TARSAL JOINT
hock

STERNEBRAE

TIBIA

ULNA

RADIUS

FIBULA

METACARPALS
front pastern

CARPAL JOINT

METATARSALS
rear pastern

PHALANGES PEDIS
toes

R PE

PHALANGES MANIS
toes

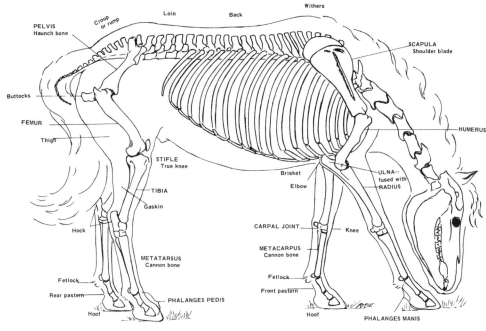

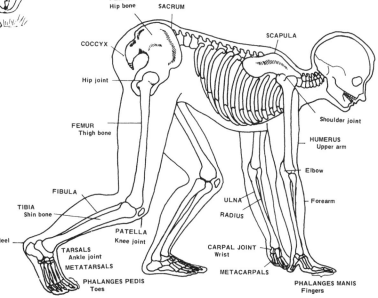

Evolution has changed the horse into a weight-carrying animal, chiefly by altering his legs from the hock and knee down. He used to walk on four toes in front and three in back, but now walks on a single toe in each foot. Though there is but a semblance of some of the original bones left in his legs, the scientific names remain, and horses and dogs still share the same principles of locomotion. Notice the horse's greater number of ribs, in contrast to the dog.

Code to the gait diagrams in this book:

Front paw—  Rear paw—

Sample:

The Pace

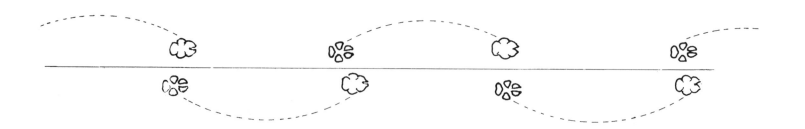

Chapter 2

Gait Patterns Described

The Natural Gaits

The term "gait" means pattern of footsteps at various rates of speed, each pattern distinguished by a particular rhythm of footfall. The **Walk**, the **Trot**, and the **Gallop** are perhaps the most commonly recognized of the gaits, but **Ambling**, **Pacing**, and **Cantering** are also normal ways in which many four-footed animals move.

The two gaits acceptable in the show ring are the walk and the trot. When a judge requests an exhibitor to "Gait your dog" he means simply that the dog be led (usually at the trot) around, across the ring and back, so that he may evaluate the dog's way of moving and how it relates to his conformation.

The Walk is a slow gait with regular beat in which the limbs move laterally—left hind, left fore, right hind, right fore. During each half stride the action is counterbalanced by triangular support with three feet on the ground at the same time. The action is subtle and quick, not to be confused with irregular patterns of footfall seen at slightly faster speeds such as the single track or amble.

The Amble is like a fast rocking walk with an *irregular four-beat cadence* in which the legs on either side move *almost*—but not quite—as a pair. This relaxed, easy movement is characteristic of a few large breeds, but all dogs amble now and then. Often seen as a transition movement between the walk and faster gaits, ambling should not be confused with pacing.

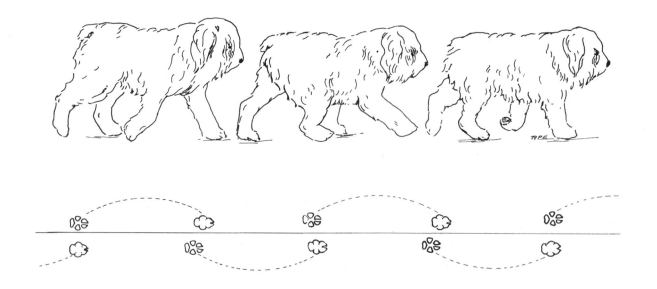

The Pace is a *two-beat lateral gait*, in which the legs on each side move back and forth exactly as a pair, causing a rolling or rocking motion of the dog's body. Structure and proportion have a direct influence on a dog's inclination to pace. This gait is characteristic of a few large breeds, but it is frowned upon in the show ring. The action is sometimes called "side-wheeling."

Early pacing horses, at first not fully appreciated for their racing potential, were dubbed "side-wheelers," a term from steamboat terminology. The long legs and great speed of modern pacers minimizes body roll.

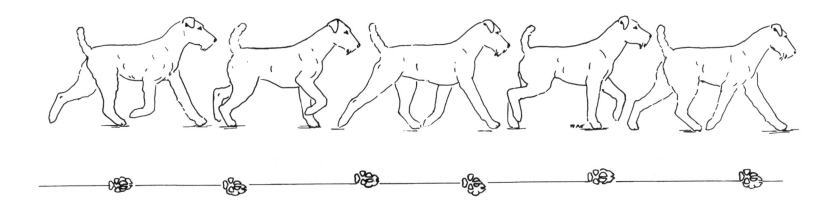

The Trot is a rhythmic two-beat gait in which diagonally opposite legs move together, i.e., right hind with left front, left hind with right front. Because only two feet are on the ground at a time the dog must rely on forward momentum for balance.

At a normal trot, when the weight is transferred from one pair of legs to the other, there is a slight almost imperceptible period of suspension as the body is propelled forward. Some people call this "spring." In a dog of the above proportions the imprints of the hind feet tend to cover the tracks left by the front.

Diagonal leg action distinguishes trotters from pacers among harness horses.

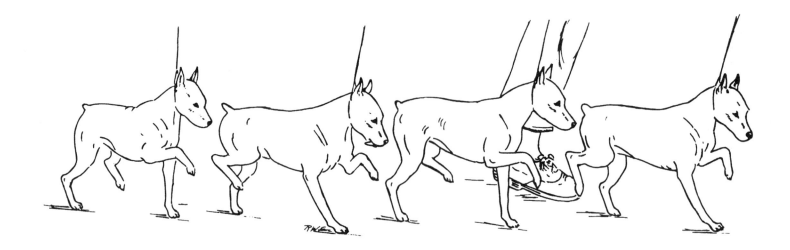

Hackney Gaiting is a unique variation of the trot. It is characterized by high, exaggerated flexion in the front and rear limbs as the forelegs lift and flex with no padding or upward flipping of the paws. Good layback of shoulder and proud head carriage, with topline remaining level as the dog moves, are basic to correct hackney action.

The term derives from hackney horses, which are bred specifically for this type of action.

12

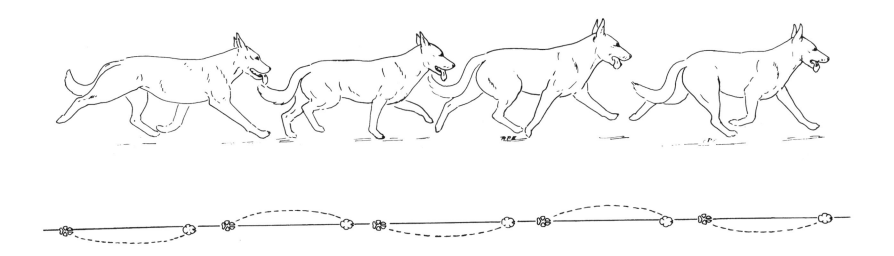

The Suspension or **Flying Trot** is a fast gait in which forward thrust contributes to a longer and more plainly discernible period of flight during each half stride. Because of the long "reach," the oncoming hind feet step beyond the imprint left by the front. Coordination and good foot timing are of great importance to avoid interference.

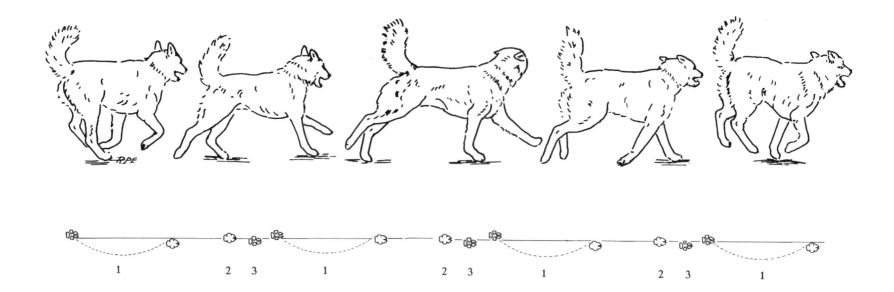

The Canter, a gait slower than the gallop and not as tiring, *has three beats to each stride*—two legs moving separately and two as a diagonal pair. When the dog "leads" with the left front foot (as in this illustration), the right foot moves simultaneously with the left rear. Cantering is sometimes referred to as the "collected gallop" or the "lope", but such references are to rate of speed rather than pattern of footfall, as they differ from the canter in this last respect.

Sound sled dogs cover the miles at a steady "lope."

The Gallop, fastest of the gaits, has *a four-beat-rhythm* and often an extra period of suspension during which the body is propelled through the air with all four feet off the ground. I have seen no better description of the gallop than the following, written by the famous canine authority, "Stonehenge":*

"Perfection of the gallop depends upon the power of extending the shoulders and forelegs as far as possible, as well as bringing the hind legs rapidly forward to give the propulsive stroke. If the hindquarters are good and well-brought into action, while the shoulders do not thrust the forelegs well forward, the action is laboured and slow. On the contrary, if the shoulders do their duty but the hind legs are not brought well forward or do not thrust the body onwards with sufficient force, the action may be elegant but it is not powerful and rapid. For these purposes, therefore, we require good shoulders, good thighs, a good back, and good legs and, lastly, for lodging the lungs and heart, whose actions are essential for the maintenance of speed, a well-formed chest."

* "Stonehenge": *The Dogs of the British Islands,* Second Edition, London 1872, p.180.

16

A combination of sound conformation, good balance, and the spirit to win, pay off as galloping race hounds near the finish line.

Chapter 3

Good Performance Is the
Test of Good Structure

Dogs that are built well can stand long days of hard work.

Good proportion lends suppleness to the back and strong thrust from hindquarters.

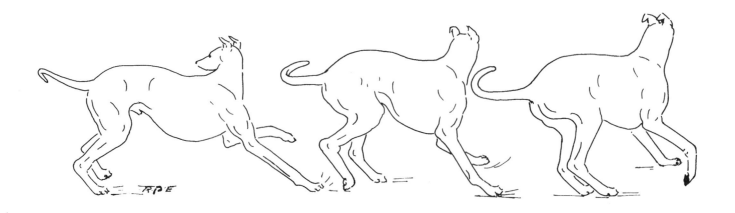

Strong pasterns and thick pads help reduce the shock of sudden impact.

A good working dog has limbs that extend freely…
and balance of body for trotting long hours without tiring.

Strong hindquarters provide strength for quick bursts of speed…

…and thrust for leaping.

Joy and enthusiasm are the keystone of performance

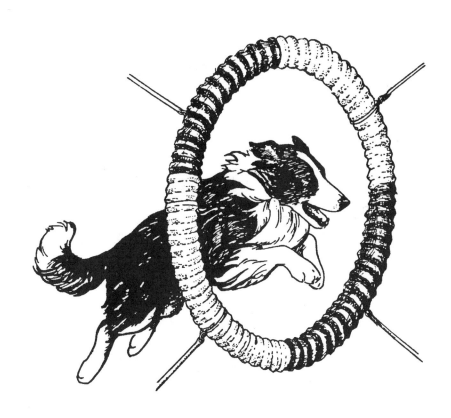

Chapter 4

Angulation and Balance
Foundation of Structure and Movement

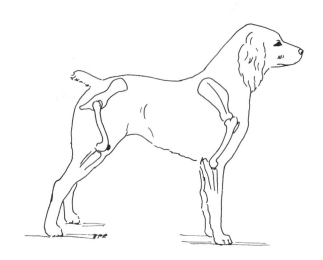

The Importance of Angulation

Essential to the appearance and qualities of endurance in all dogs are the structural features that govern balance and the ability to move freely—called "angulation." Good angulation means effortless stride and smooth action. Poor angulation tends to shorten stride, cause irregularities in gaiting patterns or make a dog's movement stilted and choppy.

Angulation has to do with the slant of the bones and size of the angles at certain joints. Those influencing structure and gait most are the shoulder and hip joints, formed by the largest, strongest joints in the dog's body. These joints counterbalance one another as they lift, open and shut with the swing of the limbs. The front of the dog normally carries 60% of the total body weight and works like a shock-absorbing mechanism as it coordinates with drive from the hindquarters and absorbs impact with the ground. Whether viewed from the side or from front or rear, the action should be smooth and harmonious with no jerking or twisting. Problems result when one part of the body has to overwork or compensate for lack of balance, injury or weakness in another.

There are generally ideal measurements for every form or figure, and authorities on canine anatomy have been no exception in drawing up standards of physical perfection for the many kinds of dogs in the world today. In each standard, the outward appearance of the breed is described, with angulation specified or implied because of its importance to overall conformation. Variations occur depending on the jobs dogs are expected to perform, and in differences within individual members of the same breed—correct or faulty. Width or depth of chest, for example, affect the relationship of the shoulder blade and the upper arm, and the angle at which they join. Length and set of the upper arm determines the position of the elbow against the chest wall. Normally the humerus should counterbalance the angle of the shoulder blade. Elbows that set too far back or too far forward can throw the front assembly out of balance and adversely affect the dog's way of moving.

Rear angulation can be influenced by the length and set of the pelvic assembly in relation to the spinal column (to which it is connected at the sacrum) and by the relative length of the leg bones. Hip joints consist of ball and socket construction with considerable rotating facility, while action of the stifles and hocks is hinge-like. These joints all share a vital role in providing strength and drive to locomotion.

Excessive angulation in any part of the dog's body is detrimental to joint support and endurance. It is never a question of the more angulation the better—it is a matter of just how much is needed for functional efficiency.

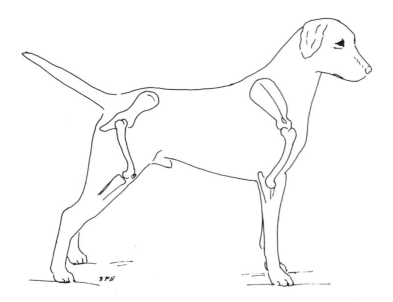

Good Angulation facilitates a smooth, ground-covering stride. Balance facilitates good foot-timing. Joints that control movement should flex easily and smoothly, providing strong thrust from the rear with spring and resilience in the forehand. The swing and extension of the forelegs should coordinate with action of the rear so that there will be no over-stepping or interfering. As a general rule, the feet should move rather close to the ground so as to avoid excessive bending of the joints, which can be inefficient and tiring.

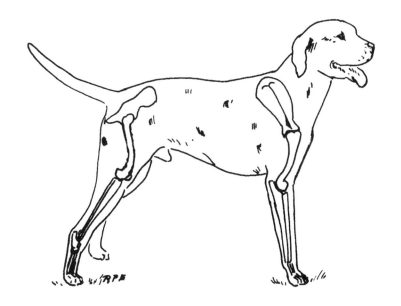

Poor Angulation shortens stride because the bones meeting at the shoulder joints and hips are steeply set, forming joints with wide open angles. Swing of the blades and the upper arms is restricted, as is bend and thrust from the rear. Dogs so constructed must take shorter steps, and their action is bouncing rather than smooth. This dog is too straight, both front and rear, but in spite of this fault and a short stilted gait, his body appears to be in balance and he may be better off than a dog lacking balance, where one end has to compensate for faultiness in the other.

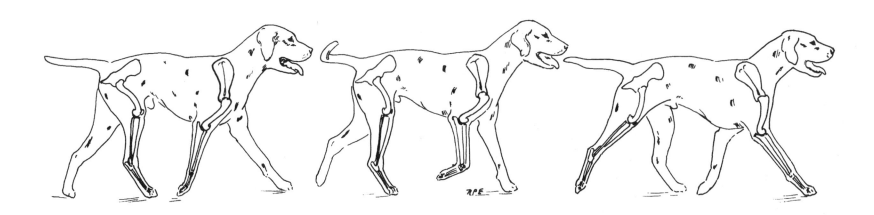

Estimating Angulation

When one talks about angles and bone lengths in a live dog, it is important to realize that there can be no exact determination. Figures are only approximate and judgments vary depending on who does the measuring, how it is done, and which bone prominences are used as landmarks. Muscles are never stable and appearances may change through handling, training, and general condition. Even as a dog stands naturally, the slightest shift in posture or turn of the head can alter the picture. However, in spite of such uncertainties, dog fanciers will no doubt always attempt to assess angulation by means of measuring tools. A goniometer is a handy instrument for this purpose. Such efforts will at least serve to train the eye in what to look for, or the hands in what to feel for.

Front Quarters

A common method for evaluating slant and placement of the bones in the front assembly is to take a line from the uppermost edge of the scapula (A) to the foremost prominence of the humerus (B) and go from there to the elbow (E). As a general rule, the distance between these points of reference should look or feel about equal, and if the front is balanced the elbow will set approximately on or close to an imaginary vertical line dropped from the caudal, or posterior, angle of the blade (C). These are not actual bone measurements, only landmarks that can be easily palpated. It is important that the dog stand naturally with its legs perpendicular to the ground.

Another way to assess angulation is to feel the scapula ridge that runs up the near center of the blade and figure the angle of an imaginary vertical line dropped from the upper tip to the ground. The slant of the humerus may be determined by a line from its upper center (D) to its lowest end (G), not to the elbow. These measurements will differ from those taken by the method described above, but the findings are more realistic as to the actual bone placement and joint angulation.

Note that a line extended upward along the scapula ridge concurs with the apex of T-2, which is the second of the nine thoracic spines (*spinous processes*) that form the withers. While slight variation may occur between T-1 and T-3, depending on conformation or shift in body posture, radiographic studies reveal T-2 as the normal location for the upper tip of the scapula in the average dog.

The dotted line A-L shows how a slope of 45 degrees would set the scapula at such an angle as to place the shoulder joint in advance of the breastbone where the entire assembly would lack muscular support of the chest wall, and the joint itself would not have such strong bracing. (See also page 70.) The text explains later why from such a position the lift and inward swing of the blade would tend to interfere with the cervical structures.

Hindquarters

In the hindquarters, length of the croup and bend of stifle and hock are more clearly visible, or at least are easy to feel under a heavy coat. However, variables in measurement can occur here as well, depending on how the dog stands; he may be crouching due to uneasiness or standing roached because of discomfort. Length and slope of the pelvic assembly can be approximated by taking a line from the forward edge of the ilium (I) to the ischium, or buttock (J). However, the exact location of the point of the buttock can be misleading because its shape and tilt may differ with the type of dog.

Pelvic slope and outline of the croup are not one and the same. While the outline of the croup and set-on of the tail may be influenced by slant of the pelvis, the outline seems to be more directly affected by the arch, dip or straightness of the lumbar section, together with the way the sacro-iliac bones attach to the wings of the ilium. The dog's tail is but a continuation of the spine.

In these diagrams, angulation in the front assembly is figured off a vertical line. Slope of the pelvis is determined off the horizontal.

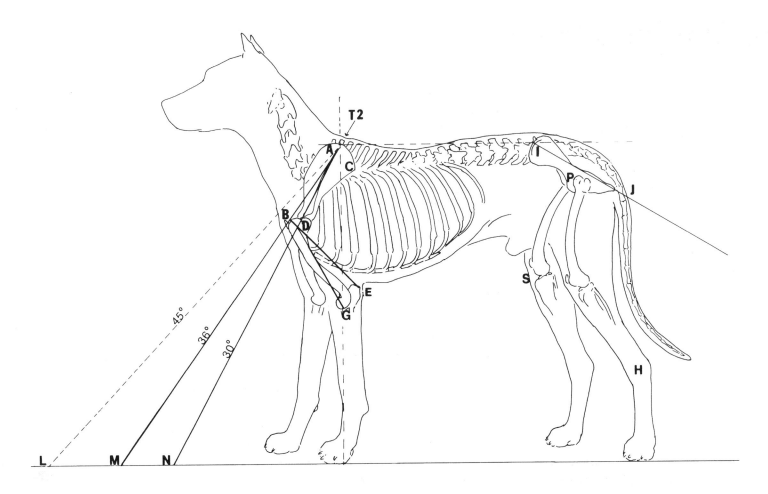

Variations in skeletal framework relate to the work dogs have been bred to do, to man's emphasis on the exotic rather than functional soundness, or to indifference with working structure through injudicious breeding programs. A dog's qualifications must be clearly understood, for differences in angulation, both front or rear, are reflected in gaiting styles as well as in quality of performance. In the above diagram, notice how the hypothetical 45 degree layback of the shoulder blade would set the shoulder joint in advance of the manubrium (forechest) where there would be no support of the ribs, and any upward swing would cause interference with cervical musculature.

The Value of Balance

Balance depends not only on the proportion of head to neck, depth of chest to length of legs and overall length of body to height, but also on a front end that matches the rear. In other words, when a dog is standing naturally the angulation at the shoulder and hip joints should be approximately equal, in order to provide the same amount of reach in the forelegs as in the rear.

A dog is not in balance if the shoulder and upper arm are steeply set and the hindquarters are well-angulated, because he will have a short stride in front and a long stride in the rear. Conversely, he is not in balance if the front is well-angulated but the hindquarters are steep, because this will mean good reach in front but a shorter stride in the rear—and the front quarters will overwork. It is possible for a dog that is equally steep fore and aft to be in balance—and he may be better off than one that lacks balance—but he will not have the quality of movement that is achieved when balance is combined with good angulation.

Lack of structural balance is the reason for much incorrect gaiting. A few illustrations of this point may be seen on the next several pages.

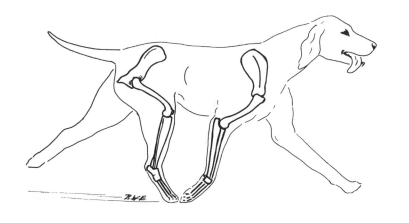

Balanced Trot
The well-balanced trot shows an almost imperceptible delay in the diagonal rhythm as the forepaws land gently, minimizing impact as the front assembly absorbs drive from the rear. This should not be confused with padding, nor should there be any overreaching or sidestepping.

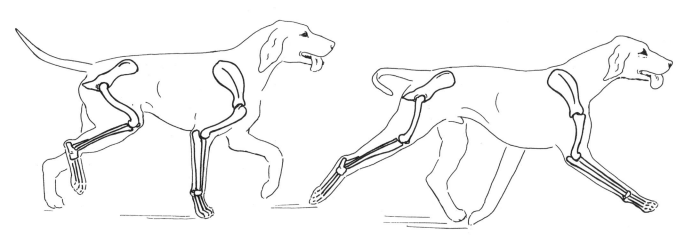

"Practically the whole propelling force of the hind limb is dependent on the ability of the dog to straighten the leg from the state of angulation to complete extension, as forcibly and as rapidly as may be required. This is dependent entirely upon the muscle power of a well-developed second thigh."
—Smythe: *Conformation of the Dog.*

Sickle Hocks (fault)

Contrasting with the suppleness of the dog on the previous page is this one with "sickle hocks". The term is derived from the sickle, a farm tool with a rigid angle where the handle meets the blade. Sickle-hocked action is stiff and shuffling, with limited use of the hock joint in forward propulsion. A sickle-hocked dog usually stands with the rear pasterns angled slightly forward, "standing under himself" to support weak hindquarters. In this illustration, the front quarters are very straight, and because of restricted push from behind, most of his energy is spent bobbing up and down—as indicated by the topline!

Sickle Hocks "Trotting behind himself" (fault)

Above is another example of sickle hocks, due to structural imbalance in a dog with steep shoulders, short body, and disproportionate length of bones in the hindquarters. For better support, he stands with the rear pasterns tucked under him. On the right, the same dog is artificially posed with the hind legs extended way back, dropping the topline and weakening the angles of support. When moving, this serious fault of over-angulation causes the dog to *"trot behind himself,"* with more rearward than forward swing of the hind legs.

This same dog illustrates also the fault of **Padding**, a compensating action in which forelimb extension is high and restricted. This is a delaying action that minimizes jarring in the front quarters when a straight front is subjected to overdrive from the rear.

Pounding (fault)

"**Pounding**" is another gaiting fault which results from the dog's stride being shorter in front than in the rear. The forefeet strike the ground before the rear stride is expended. If a dog with this fault does nothing to spare himself, such as "padding", "hackneying" or pacing, the thrust from the hindquarters causes the front feet to hit the ground hard, as happens when a person is pushed suddenly and is forced to take a quick step before his joints can properly "give" to cushion the impact. In the dog, such impact has a pile-driving effect through pasterns and shoulder bones, causing abrupt, choppy action at the withers. Constant "pounding" tends to bruise joint cartilage and may eventually cause the dog to "break down in front."

Overreaching and Padding (faults)

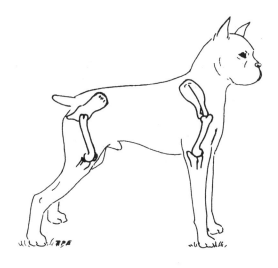

Overreaching at the trot is usually caused by more angulation and drive from behind than the front quarters can easily accommodate. The rear paws are forced to step to one side of the front to avoid interfering or clipping. This is one of the many forms of poor foot timing, but it must not be confused with the natural overreach seen in the suspension trot, the canter or gallop. The exaggerated lift of the forelimbs in this illustration is called **Padding**.

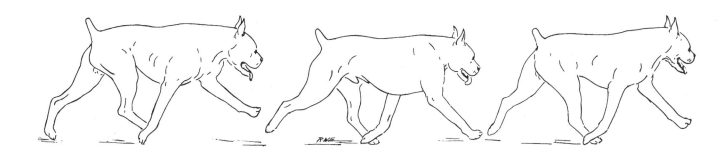

"Overreaching" Due to More Height than Length (fault)

Puppies often **Overreach** as they develop through leggy stages when height at the withers may exceed length from buttock to shoulder joint by a fractional difference. Interesting action is illustrated here in that this young dog places his right hind paw first to the outside of the front leg, then to the inside, in the effort to avoid interference. He is also **Padding**, which means that the forelimbs extend too high, throwing the landing phase of the paws out of rhythm with expended thrust from the rear. Attractive as this pup is, he will always lack structural balance because there is more angulation in the rear quarters than in the front.

Pacing to Avoid Interference (fault)

Generally speaking, dogs need a little more length of body than height at the withers, in order to be able to coordinate drive from the rear with reach in the front. A dog that is too short usually lacks angulation in one end or the other and often in both. Sometimes, if rear angulation is better, he may become a habitual pacer (as illustrated above) to keep the hind feet from stepping on the front.

Illustrated below is the same dog trotting awkwardly as the rear legs have to by-pass the front. This is an extreme example of poor foot timing.

Overreaching

Pacing as a Result of "Square" Body Structure

Mature dogs that are "squarely" built, but tend to stand a bit lower at the withers than at the croup, often develop a natural tendency to avoid leg interference by pacing, rather than trotting. In the lateral action the body tends to roll as the dog shifts his weight from side to side.

The dog in these illustrations is a natural pacer. In the top sequence, he is pacing easily. In the sequence below he is trotting awkwardly because he is forced to "crab" to avoid leg interference. Pacing is frowned upon in the show ring, regardless of breed.

Hackney Action as a Fault

Hackney Action *as a fault* is caused by more drive from the rear than the front can take. To avoid interference, the dog resorts to a quick, extra high lift and extension of the front legs in a delaying action before landing. This is called **padding**. The movement is bouncy rather than smooth, as evidenced by the tips of this little dog's ears, which flip up and down with each step. Cute as it may appear to ringside spectators, hackneying as a fault is a waste of energy (sometimes caused by a tight lead!) and very tiring. It should not be confused with acceptable hackney action characteristic of a few small breeds. (See page 12.)

The well balanced natural trot is rhythmic and effortless.

Good Front Pasterns

Strong Pasterns almost invariably keep company with good fronts because they are part of the bone assembly that receives and cushions impact with the ground. Good pasterns and strong carpal joints have kinetic spring and resilience.

"Knuckling Over" (fault)

"Knuckling over" in the carpal joint is sometimes referred to as "over at the knees." Technically, this is known as hyperextension of the carpal joint. It is a serious fault that throws the front quarters out of balance. The expression "knuckling over" is also used in reference to hyperextension of the hock.

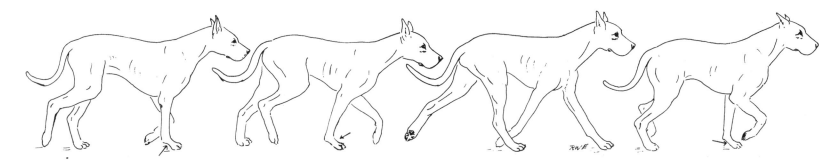

"Broken Pasterns" and "Overreaching" *(faults)*

A straight front with low withers forces this dog to land heavily with each step. Constant pounding has weakened ligaments and tendons in the pasterns to the point where they bend far too much as the dog's weight passes over the front quarters. Also called "down at the pasterns."

41

How Angulation Affects Muscle Structure

In the preceding pages, angulation has been discussed as it relates to length of stride and to balance. Another important consideration is how it affects muscle structure.

Dog "A" illustrates how good angulation gives wider spread to the muscles, due to the fact that the shoulder bones and the pelvis are properly slanted. This slant seems to provide more area for muscle attachment and lends strength and substance to the dog's appearance. Good angulation also goes hand-in-hand with a strong middle piece, and a rib cage that extends well back.

Correct placement of the scapula, called "good shoulder layback," contributes to Dog "A's" reach of neck and good head carriage, and gives the neckline a pleasing transition into the withers and topline. In conformation terms, this is referred to as a neck "well-set-on" or "setting well into the shoulders."

Dog "B's" upright structure in both front and rear quarters illustrates how poor angulation tends to reduce the size and slant of the bones and affects the area of muscle attachment. In this type of dog these bones are usually narrower, with the muscles relatively poorly developed, and it may be said the dog "lacks substance." In addition, steep shoulders detract from the dog's overall appearance because the neckline joins the withers abruptly and tends to make the neck look short.

Dotted lines in these two studies call attention to differences in width across front and rear quarters, and show at a glance that the dog with greater width has better angulation. Correct positioning of the shoulder and pelvis always lends breadth to the quarters (viewed in profile), from shoulder joint to a line dropped just behind the blade, and from the forward edge of the pelvis to the buttocks. It is such structure that clues us in to the better movers, whatever the breed of dog, for the principles and advantages of good angulation are the same for all.

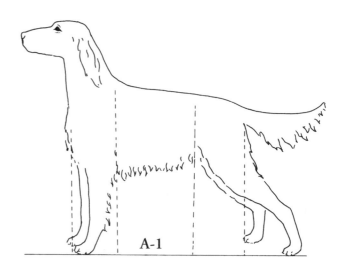

A-1

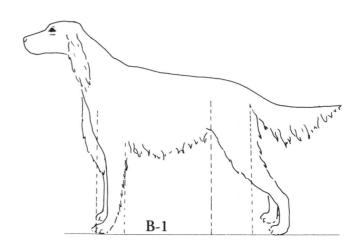

B-1

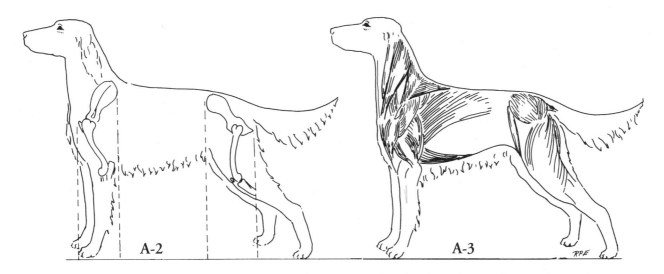

Dog "A" — Illustrating how good angulation provides the foundation for good muscle structure, lending breadth to the front and rear quarters and substance to the overall picture.

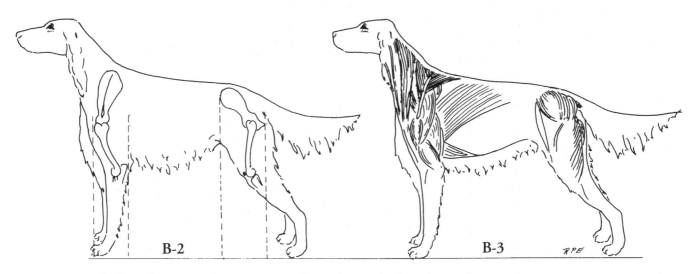

Dog "B" — Illustrating how poor angulation limits the foundation for muscle structure, narrowing the width across front and rear quarters, and giving the appearance of less substance.

Major Muscles

It takes many muscles working together to produce sound movement. Here is what some of them do.

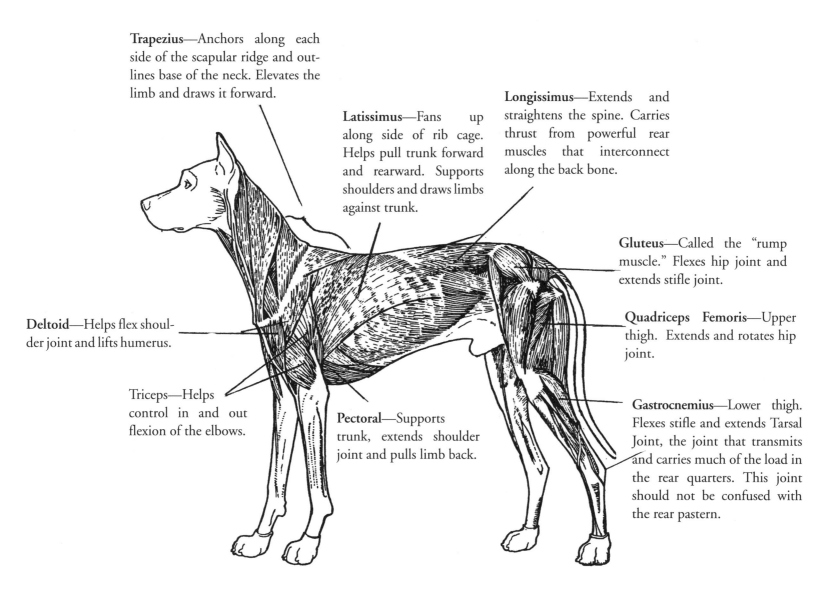

Trapezius—Anchors along each side of the scapular ridge and outlines base of the neck. Elevates the limb and draws it forward.

Latissimus—Fans up along side of rib cage. Helps pull trunk forward and rearward. Supports shoulders and draws limbs against trunk.

Longissimus—Extends and straightens the spine. Carries thrust from powerful rear muscles that interconnect along the back bone.

Gluteus—Called the "rump muscle." Flexes hip joint and extends stifle joint.

Deltoid—Helps flex shoulder joint and lifts humerus.

Quadriceps Femoris—Upper thigh. Extends and rotates hip joint.

Triceps—Helps control in and out flexion of the elbows.

Pectoral—Supports trunk, extends shoulder joint and pulls limb back.

Gastrocnemius—Lower thigh. Flexes stifle and extends Tarsal Joint, the joint that transmits and carries much of the load in the rear quarters. This joint should not be confused with the rear pastern.

The Importance of Flexibility for Top Performance

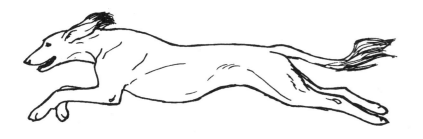

A firmly muscled, flexible back, clearly displayed in the performance of dogs bred for speed, is no less critical for the folding and stretching that is helpful in activities of all kinds.

Chapter 5

A Word About Toplines and Tailsets

A Strong Vertebral Column is Essential for Enduring Performance

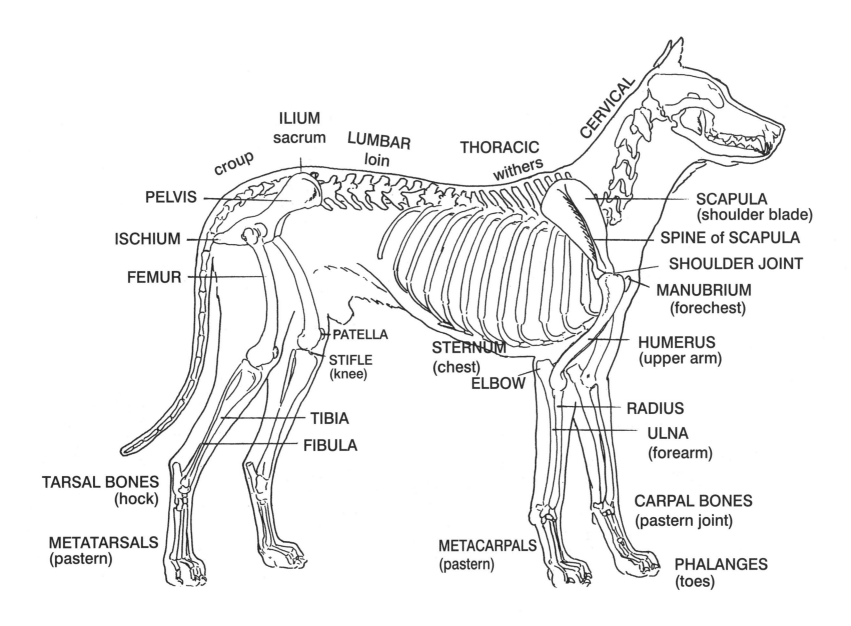

ILIUM
sacrum
LUMBAR
loin
THORACIC
withers
CERVICAL
croup
PELVIS
ISCHIUM
FEMUR
PATELLA
STIFLE
(knee)
STERNUM
(chest)
ELBOW
TIBIA
FIBULA
TARSAL BONES
(hock)
METATARSALS
(pastern)
METACARPALS
(pastern)
SCAPULA
(shoulder blade)
SPINE of SCAPULA
SHOULDER JOINT
MANUBRIUM
(forechest)
HUMERUS
(upper arm)
RADIUS
ULNA
(forearm)
CARPAL BONES
(pastern joint)
PHALANGES
(toes)

Variations in Toplines

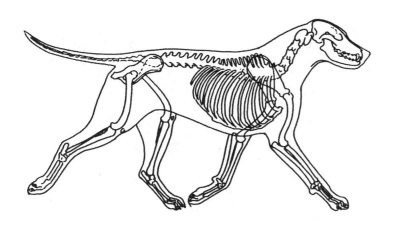

The structure of the spine, whether the topline is level, moderately arched, or prominently curved, has a direct bearing on outline of the croup, slope of the pelvis, and set-on of the tail.

Whatever the variance in type, the ribcage should extend well back from forechest to last rib to give adequate room for the heart and lungs. Good length to the ribcage also provides maximum support to the central body and contributes to smooth transition of drive from rear quarters into the front. A dog's running gear is attached to the spine only at the sacrum between the upper wings of the pelvis. In the front assembly, since there is no collar bone, muscular support alone helps stabilize the shoulders against the spine and chest wall.

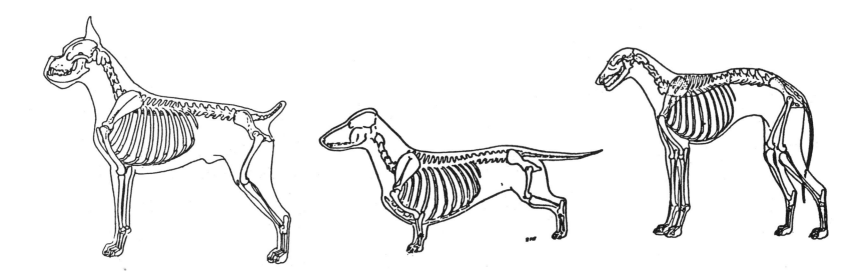

Roach and Pacing (faults)

An exaggerated arch that extends from base of the neck to tail is called a Roach. The back is stiff with downward pitch to the croup. Though the problem may be genetic, it is often caused by injury, physical stress or illness. Gait is restricted as the dog moves the best way he can to relieve discomfort. Both these subjects are pacing.

Roaching Due to Physical Stress

This sketch was drawn from a photograph of exhausted sled dogs as they neared the finish line of a race, most of them pacing or ambling to rest muscles weary from trotting and cantering. Here the pace and amble are rightly referred to as "fatigue" gaits. The backs are roached as the dogs switch to lateral movement to relieve physical stress.

The Sway Back (fault)

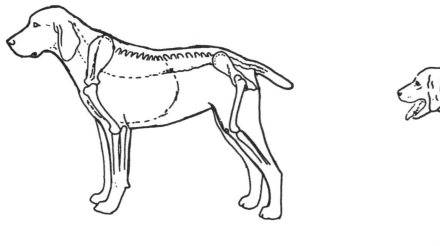 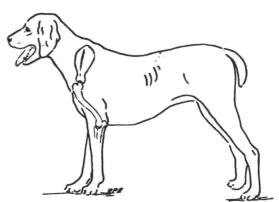

In contrast to the roached spine is the backbone that dips in the middle causing the lumbar vertebrae to tilt upward through the sacrum into a croup that may be higher than the withers. The mid-section is weak, resulting in too much flexion throughout the topline with side to side rocking in the rear quarters as the dog moves.

 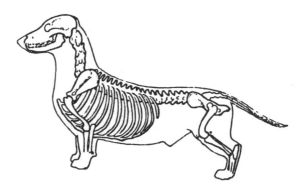

51

"Running Down Hill"—the high croup (fault)

When the croup is higher than the withers a dog may give the appearance of "running down hill," placing undue strain on the front quarters.

Seen from the side, this subject clearly illustrates an undesirable topline as the high rear drives into the front quarters. As a result the dog **Pads** and the pasterns flip up to soften impact with the ground.

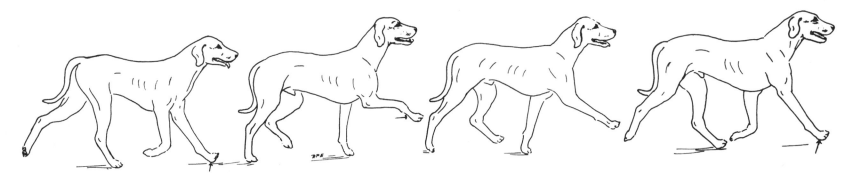

Faulty Topline—"Running Downhill"

Youth may have its problems. Some puppies seem to develop faster in the rear end than in the front, which gives them the appearance of "running down hill." Long dogs with short legs never have to cope with the inconvenience of rear feet overstepping the front, but lack of structural balance still impairs symmetry and overall quality.

Good level topline

Necklines—What They Tell

Good Necklines

Two illustrations showing what is meant by "neck well set on." Good necklines merge gradually with strong withers at the base of the neck and form a pleasing transition into the back. The slightest shift in leg position can alter the appearance of the front assembly.

Faulty Necklines

Flat Withers usually indicate upright shoulder blades, creating an abrupt juncture at the base of the neck, and the neckline appears short. Long-haired dogs are sometimes groomed to disguise faulty fronts, but actual lay of the scapula can be determined by feeling for it. Horsemen who know structure avoid animals with steep shoulders and flat withers, not only because upright blades mean a hard pounding ride, but also because flat withers let the saddle slide forward.

1

A neck of good length, well set into a working shoulder assembly, lends greater ease for tracking, retrieving and carrying.

Tails—and What They Tell

"Even as the dog begins with his head he ends with his tail and by it many a story is told, for it expresses health, mental attitude, and what may be expected in the rest of the spinal column. Beware of any type tail that is not normally characteristic of the specific breed."
—Lyon, McDowell, *The Dog in Action, 1950*

"I like the one on the left," said the judge, "because he has more behind the tail."

Notice the tailset of the dog below (left). The lower end of the pelvis (ischium) extends well behind the base of the tail, indicating good breadth to the hindquarters and contributing to a strong topline. The subject also shows a pleasing neckline merging gradually into well set shoulders. There is less slope to the humerus, however, which sets the elbow a bit further forward. While this feature is undesirable in many breeds, it is characteristic of "squarely built" terriers. The good conformation of this dog in both front and rear quarters gives rise to the old horseman's expression, "built like a cleverly made hunter, short in the back but standing over a lot of ground."

By contrast, the dog on the right has a short neckline with abrupt juncture at the withers. The tail sets directly over the lower end of the pelvis, partner to narrow hindquarters and undesirable length to the back.

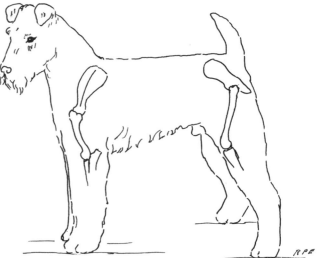

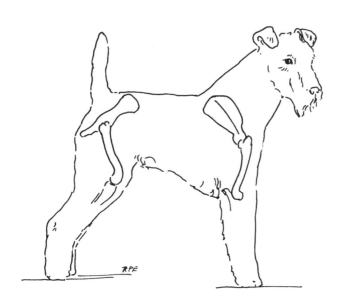

58

Tails help with balance

Often referred to as a continuation of the spine, the tail tells much, not only about temperament but how a dog relies on the swing of his tail—or just a wiggle of the rump—for balance. There are short tails, docked tails, long tails, curly tails, crooked tails, high and low set tails, merry tails, dignified tails and sad tails. All are needed for kinetic balance, whether the dog is tearing around with playmates, making sharp turns, climbing, jumping, swimming, racing, or standing on point in the hunting field. Slight differences in slope and length of the pelvis affect outline of the croup, set of the tail, and may be correct or incorrect within members of the same breed.

These sketches, one drawn as we look down on the back, the other from the side, show how subtle adjustments of the spine and swing of the tail help to counterbalance lateral flexion as the dog walks on a narrow beam.

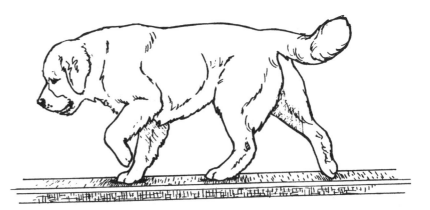

59

Flexibility in the spine, both lateral and vertical,
means greater ease in performance

—though some seem to do pretty well
without it!

Chapter 6

Understanding Fronts

An Inside Look

Function Influences Form

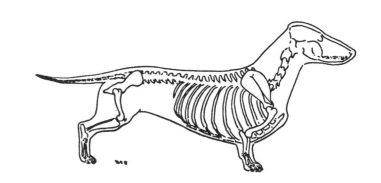

Here is a variety of dog developed through selective breeding to ferret pests from underground. The elbows are set above the line of the sternum (lower chest), a feature that frees the elbows for digging, while the dog's weight rests mainly on his chest. The long gradual upward slant of the sternum helps him to slide more easily over rocks and roots—a handy arrangement in case a speedy retreat is called for.

Three Comparative Types of Front Assemblies

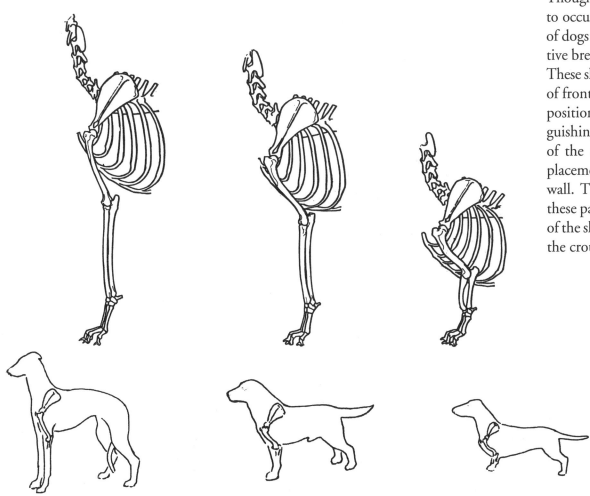

Though countless variations in structure continue to occur through genetic mixtures, specific types of dogs have survived through centuries of selective breeding to meet our needs and preferences. These skeletal diagrams illustrate three basic kinds of front assemblies. While each indicates a good position and slope of the shoulder blade, distinguishing features reveal differences in angulation of the shoulder joint, set of the humerus and placement of the elbow in relation to the chest wall. The following page shows illustrations of these particular types showing not only structure of the shoulders, but also differences in outline of the croups and rear assemblies.

A. Greyhound

This foreassembly is designed primarily for speed, with wide angle at the shoulder joint, a sharply descending humerus and elbow set below the sternum. The sharply descending croup lends flexion in bringing the hind legs well forward under the body for maximum propulsion and rear extension when galloping

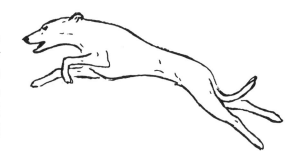

B. German Shepherd/Retriever

Strong fronts are needed for herding, retrieving, carrying, tracking, draft work and other purposes. This calls for a humerus long enough to set the elbow back under the highest point of the shoulder blade to provide maximum area for muscle attachment. A good foreassembly balanced with normal angulation in the rear quarters contributes to even movement and ease over fences.

C. Corgi/Bassett

The achondroplastic structure—seen in numerous dogs bred down in size—shows limbs foreshortened with bones frequently bowed.

64

This type of farm dog will drive a herd of cows and should be able to dodge kicking heels because of its low frame.

Cineradiography Casts New Light on a Much Discussed Subject

There seems to be more misunderstanding about the front structure of a dog than of any other part of its anatomy, probably because the bones making up the fore assembly are not visible to the naked eye, nor clearly pictured through feel. In the Introduction of this edition I mentioned that my search for answers to questions that have long puzzled me led to a study of bone and joint motion at Harvard University's Museum of Comparative Zoology, where specially designed equipment makes possible the simultaneous photographing and fluoroscoping of dogs as they move on a treadmill.

The technique is known as **cineradiography**. Taken on 16mm film, the results are similar to moving X-rays, which reveal the dog's remarkable skeletal machinery from the side as well as from underneath the body.

Dogs representing a variety of type and conformation were used in the survey. Except at the gallop, the subjects moved on the treadmill at average trotting speed. In addition to the cineradiography, a number of still X-rays were taken of dogs in standing position, rather than lying on their side, to show the natural setting of the shoulder assembly as it bears the weight of the trunk. The radiographic findings take the guesswork out of what really goes on and challenge some long standing notions.

Tracing from single 16mm movie frame of a Collie moving at a moderate trot. Dotted lines indicate free excursion of the shoulder assembly as the blades swing from their upper edges. At a moderate trot, the excursion (lift and fall) of the blades is about 30 degrees.

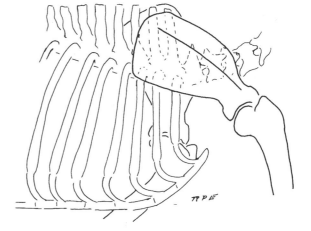

At the gallop, the excursion is much greater.

The Myth and Facts About Shoulder Structure

There is a human tendency to accept what appears in print as having withstood some incredible truth test. A case in point is the long held belief that a 45-degree slope of the shoulder blade is necessary for providing maximum extension or reach of the forelimb, and this is written into many breed standards. I have often wondered about the illusiveness of this detail, for I have never found it myself, and it was not until given the opportunity to observe skeletal action through cineradiography that I realized why such a position would be a mechanical impossibility to the dog's function. A 45-degree slant, or layback, would be workable if the blade were a stationary bone with a more or less fixed joint from which the upper arm moved forward and back. Actually, this is not the case.

What we have failed to recognize is the great mobility of the shoulder blade as partner to the action of the upper arm, which serves as a lever in lifting and transporting the central body forward as smoothly as possible.

At a moderate trot, the blade swings from its upper rim with an excursion, lift and fall of about 30 degrees. At the gallop, the excursion is much greater. (*See drawings, previous page.*) As the assembly lifts, it also swings inward, leaving the supportive role of the chest wall. If the motion **began** from a 45-degree position, the scapula would lift too high and the "medial component of the shoulder musculature would force the shoulder to bear directly on cervical structures." (F.A. Jenkins).

Radiographic studies show that as a dog stands with the forelegs in natural pose, a blade that sets about 30 degrees off a vertical plane—measured up the scapular ridge—is within normal limits for the average well-built dog. We must try to visualize the anatomical limitations within which the shoulder and upper arm are held against the ribcage and the way in which chest shape and muscling influence the position of both. The combined factors not only influence shoulder excursion but also explain why a dog tends to single track or move with a wider footfall.

The humerus is a strong bone shaft, normally longer than the scapula, that slopes down and back into the elbow. Its position and relationship with the shoulder blade varies with functional type and may be correct or faulty within members of the same breed. The differences influence angulation and placement of the elbow against the chest wall and, as previously stated, are reflected in particular gaiting styles and in the quality of performance.

The following discussion in no way lessens the importance of good shoulder layback; it is directed toward a clearer understanding of what constitutes a normal front and how the assembly functions as a whole.

Shoulder Position

Because the dog has no collarbone, full muscular support of the chest wall is needed when the dog is at rest and for control of the limbs when in motion. **Many differences occur in the way dogs are built but in each one the ligaments, tendons and muscles originate and insert on the same anatomical parts, and accordingly establish the boundaries within which the scapula is positioned against the chest wall.** Normally, the blade's lower edge joins the upper arm at the joint just back of the breastbone, and from there it slants inward toward the spinous processes that form the withers. The trapezius muscles that flow forward over the lower neck and rearward over the back anchor on either side of the scapular spine. These play a vital role in holding the shoulder blades in place, and in lifting and retracting the blades as the dog moves.

Index to Facing Page

A – acromion (point of shoulder)
C – cervical (neck)
E – elbow
F – sternum
f – sternebrae
H – humerus (upper arm)
L – lumbar vertebrae
M – manubrium (breastbone)
P – pelvis
S – scapula (shoulder blade)
s – scapular spine (or ridge)
T – spinous process of the thoracic vertebrae
  (9 in all, forming the withers)

In reference to the degree of angulation in the front assembly measurements are determined off a vertical line. Slope of the pelvis is estimated off the vertical.

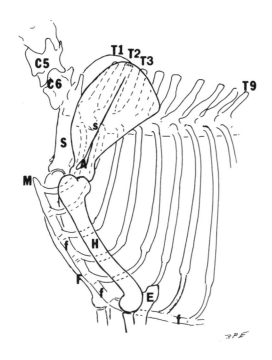

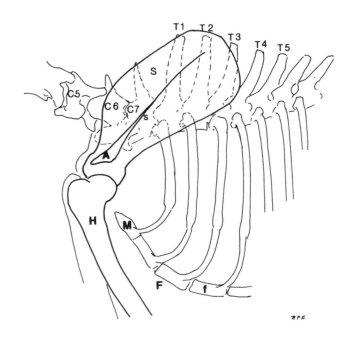

Normal Shoulder Position

Tracing from a lateral X-ray of the shoulder assembly of a dog in natural standing position, showing structure that allows optimum joint and muscular support against the chest wall. This subject has an excellent front assembly, with the scapula slanting at a desired 30-degree angle counterbalanced by a correctly set humerus and elbow. (Note: The collie that was the subject of this tracing is shown trotting on page 67.)

Unnatural Shoulder Position

Tracing from a lateral X-ray of a dog lying on its side with the scapula pulled forward to simulate a 45-degree layback of the shoulder blade. The upper tip of the ridge of the blade (the scapular spine) is in the area of T-2 where the trapezius and rhomboideus muscles normally hold it in place. However, in this illustration, the shoulder joint is forced into an unrealistic non-functional position far in advance of the breastbone, clearly showing why a 45-degree slope to the blade is a common misconception. Such a position is a mechanical impossibility for were the dog standing this way the supportive role of the thoracic wall (chest) would be absent, and, when moving, the upward swing of the blades would force the musculature to bear on the neck of the cervical structures. (Jenkins).

A Few Variables

Though the shoulder assembly is always in the same area of the dog's body, subtle differences in shape of the chest can affect its placing and the overall quality of movement. Ribcages vary in depth, length and breadth. Some have good arc and spring, some widen quickly near the forechest; others may be narrow. Variations also occur in the length and forward thrust of the individual sternebrae between the lower ribs which form the floor of the chest. Too, there may be slight diversities in height and slant of the withers, or in the vertebral lengths that separate them, however minute. All of these factors influence angulation singly or in combination.

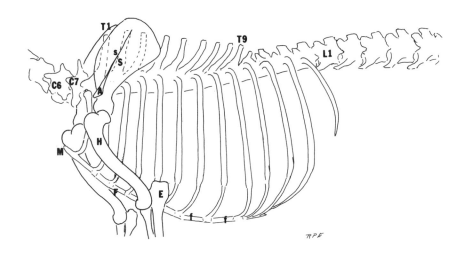

Tracing from a radiograph of a Cairn Terrier taken in standing position. Layback of the shoulder is within normal range of 30 degrees and there is balanced relationship with the humerus against the chest wall. However, the upper rims of the shoulder blades are above the apex of the withers, which in this dog indicate looseness in the front assembly. Because of roaching, the topline is poor. Notice that the roach begins at the 10th spinal vertebrae. Studies through cineradiography show this subject trotting, with physical problems quite visible. See pages 81-84.

Index

A – acromion (point of shoulder)
C – cervical (neck)
E – elbow
F – sternum
F – sternebrae
H – humerus (upper arm)
L – lumbar vertebrae
M– manubrium (breastbone)
P – pelvis
S – scapula (shoulder blade)
s – scapular spine (or ridge)
T – spinous process of the thoracic vertebrae
    (9 in all, forming the withers)

Steep Shoulder

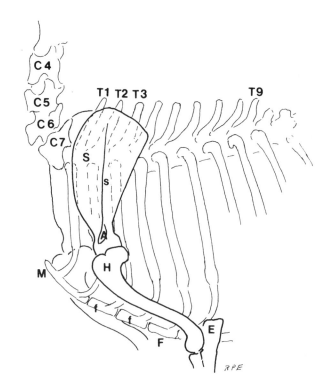

Tracing from a radiograph of a Shi Tzu in standing position. The shoulder blade is almost vertical, pointing upward toward T-1. This assembly is out of balance, giving the appearance of the dog "setting over himself." Were this little dog stripped of its coat, an abrupt juncture at the base of the neck would be clearly visible. In contrast to the diagram of the Cairn on the facing page, the upper edges of the shoulder blades set below the rise of the withers.

Pigeon Breast

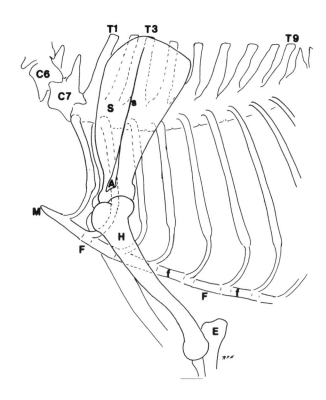

Tracing from a radiograph of a Siberian Husky taken in standing position, showing the shoulder and upper arm set too far back along a narrow, shallow chest. While some prominence of the breastbone is desirable for the attachment of the "pulley" muscles that advance the central body and control swing of the forelimbs, too much prominence gives rise to the term *pigeon breasted*.

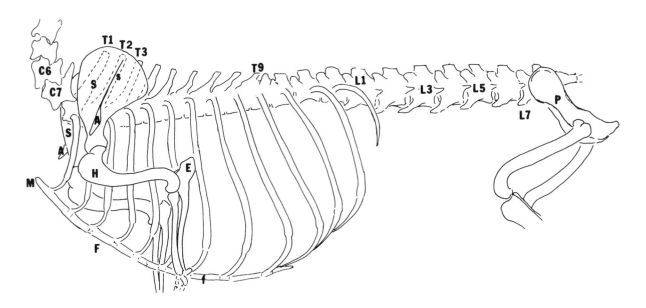

Above is a tracing from a radiograph taken in standing position. The shoulder assembly is out of balance and the chest line is abnormally low, even for this kind of achondroplastic dog. Notice the upward tilt of the ischium (buttock).

At left and right are sketches of the same Doxie, traced from 16mm movie frames. Because of faulty placement of the elbows, the upper arms cannot coordinate efficiently with the blades, and the legs therefore swing outward more than forward, resulting in **paddling** and **padding**.

Paddling

Padding

Chapter 7

Mobility and Excursion of the Shoulder Assembly

The following skeletal studies of shoulder action are drawn from individual 16mm movie frames made by means of cineradiography. The diagrams show progressive phases of the front assembly functioning as a unit with slight opening and closing of the shoulder joint. Due to limited size of the camera field it was not possible to include the entire dog.

Each stride phase is correlated as closely as possible with similar positions of the dog sketched beneath. The latter studies were drawn from regular 16mm film frames.

Shoulder Movement at the Trot

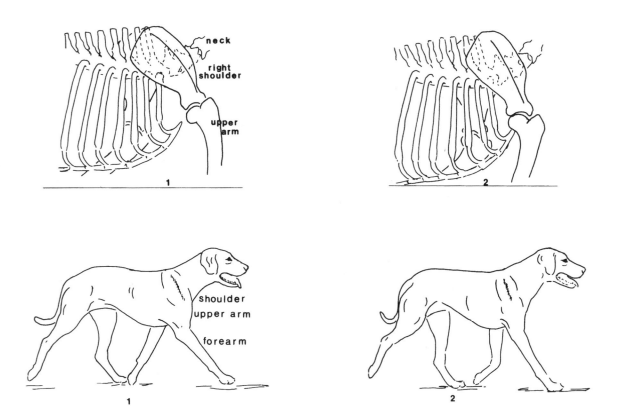

A good shoulder assembly has the flexibility to lift and fold like a shock absorbing mechanism as it absorbs impact with the ground and carries the central body smoothly forward. The upper arms serve as levers to lift the blades, which simultaneously pivot from their upper edge where they lie in against the withers. When I say "pivot" I mean a slight swiveling or elliptical motion, because the amount of movement is controlled by muscles which in turn are affected by conformation of the chest and the dog's physical condition.

Shoulder Movement at the Trot *(continued)*

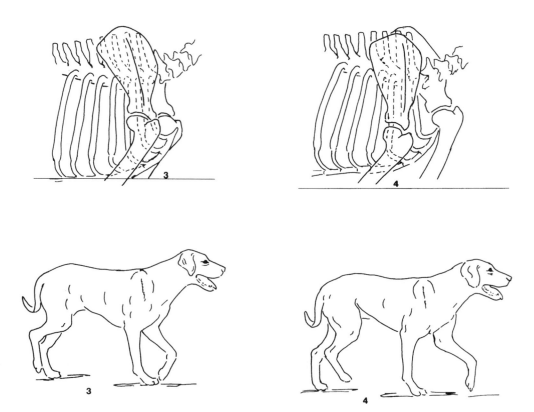

In forward motion, the shoulder loses most of the supportive role of the chest wall and must rely on muscles for stability. There is no collarbone between its lower edge and the breastbone. In the effort to maintain body balance over a central support, the medial pull of the musculature causes the limbs to swing inward over the narrowing portion of the chest. The direction of pull is indicated in the diagrams by the dark line (scapular ridge) which appears to shift as the near blade glides over the ribs. As the shoulder moves rearward, the action is slightly lateral due to the increase in spring of rib.

Shoulder Movement at the Trot *(continued)*

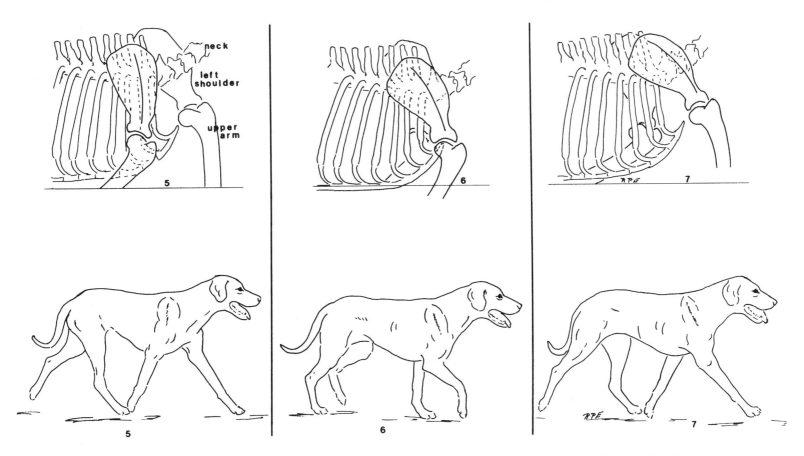

There is some undulation in the topline as drive from the rear quarters transfers weight from one diagonal pair of legs to the other when, for a split second, all four feet are off the ground (fig. 5 and 7). The brief suspension is easier to detect in some breeds than in others and among individuals within a breed. It depends in springiness of gait, quality of conformation, and soundness, and is referred to as **moving easily** or **moving heavily**.

Shoulder Movement at the Gallop

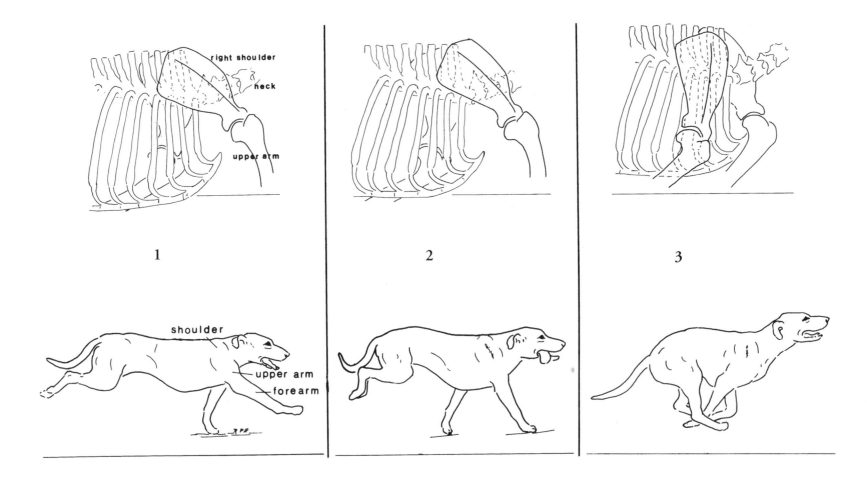

1   2   3

Shoulder excursion at the gallop is far greater than at the trot, with extreme extension of the forelimbs. The lift is emphasized by powerful leverage of the upper arms and strong rearing action in the hindquarters, which thrusts the trunk upward into the flight phases of each stride. Note baselines. Here is shown the double suspension rotary gallop in which there are two flight phases during each full stride. "Rotary" refers to the sequence of footfall.

Shoulder Movement at the Gallop *(continued)*

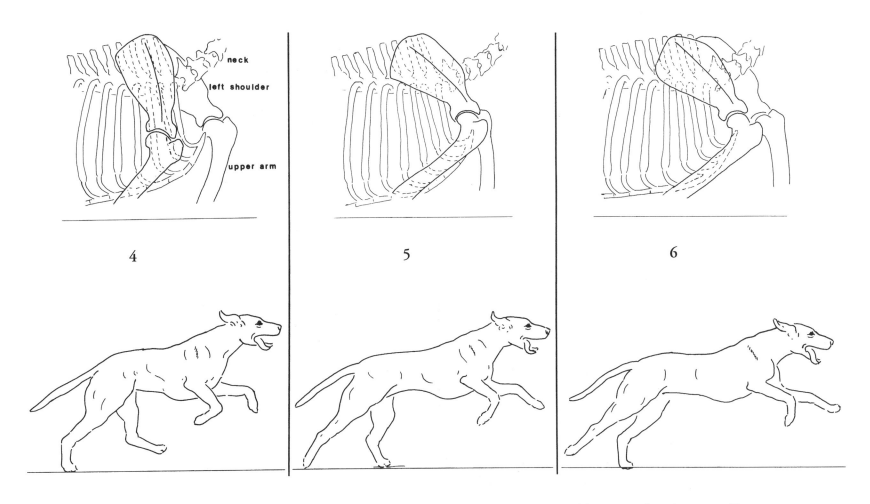

neck

left shoulder

upper arm

4

5

6

Whether trotting or galloping, correct positioning of the shoulder assembly means that the controlling muscles can serve to optimum advantage, allowing freedom of motion without excessive slipping at the withers.

Shoulder Movement at the Gallop *(continued)*

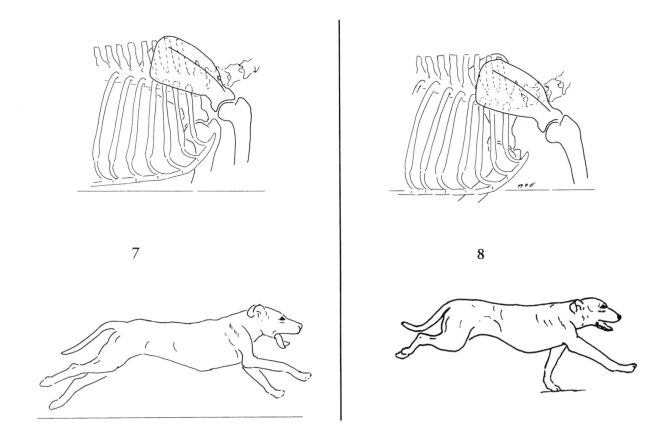

7

8

Add to this qualification a strong working back and hindquarters to balance and we have the essential ingredients for an enduring, ground-covering gait.

Loose Shoulders—What Happens Inside

The terrier shown here is the subject of the diagrams on pages 81- 86. These diagrams show excessive vertical action in the shoulders. The chest drops low within the front assembly and the upper blades rise abnormally high above the tips of the withers. A "low slung" chest is characteristic of some basic breeds, but if the conformation is faulty it hampers freedom of action. This terrier's front assembly is not balanced, reach of the forelimbs is restricted, and his padding gait causes the central body to twist and roll. We might add that poor condition can accentuate the trouble.

The subject of these diagrams also had lateral *patella luxation*, which is a slipping of the kneecap from its groove at the base of the femur. This unsoundness accentuated his gaiting problem by making the rear limbs swing outward. Patella luxation is more often medial, in which the kneecap slips inward, showing symptoms such as are illustrated on page 107.

Loose Shoulders—What Happens Inside

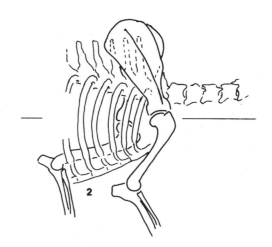

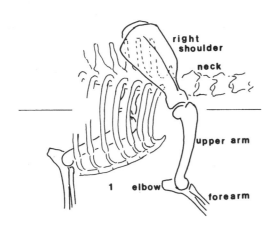

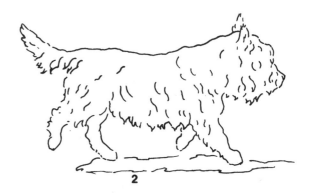

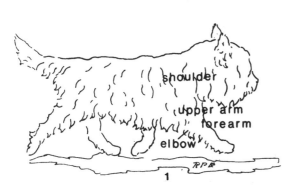

Notice how the upper blades move loosely above the withers.

Loose Shoulders—What Happens Inside *(continued)*

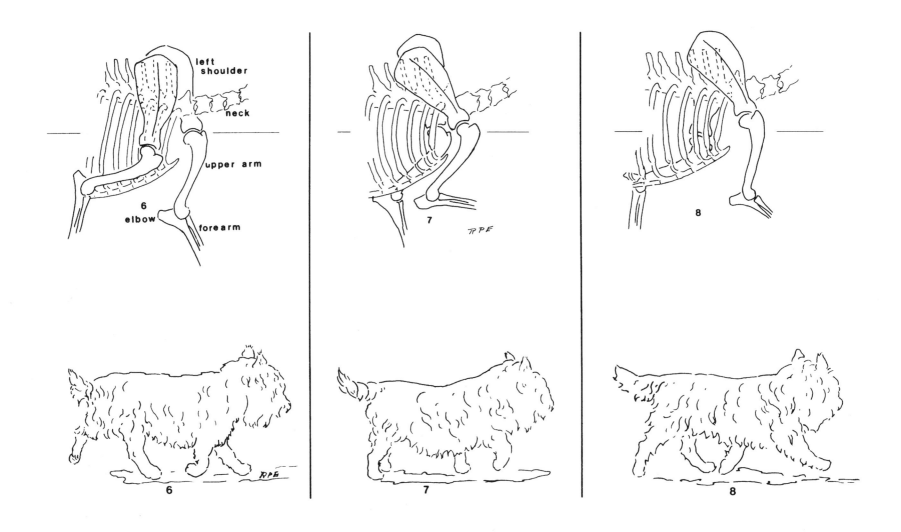

Another Look at Loose Shoulders

Faulty placement of the shoulders against the chest wall reduces muscular support needed for firm control of the limbs. These illustrations show the blades steeply set and too far forward, causing the neck to appear short. The entire shoulder assembly lacks balance, a fault that in this case causes rocking, crossing, paddling, toeing in and other departures from good movement.

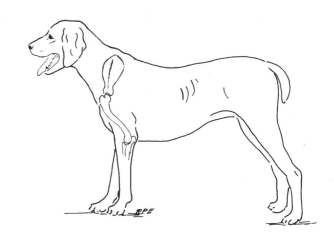

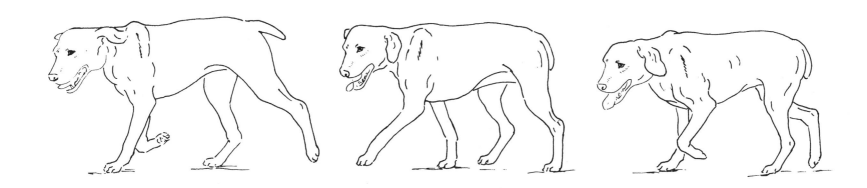

Notice the tips of the blades, which rise and drop in stilted fashion with each step. Loose shoulders do not carry the central body firmly and smoothly.

This dog has a short rib-cage and long coupling, contributing to a weak topline. This is not a working back, as much energy is lost in bouncing up and down and in twisting from side to side. The lack of quality was evident as a young puppy.

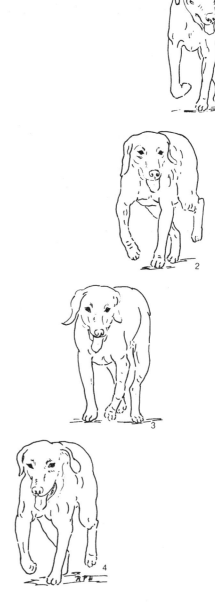

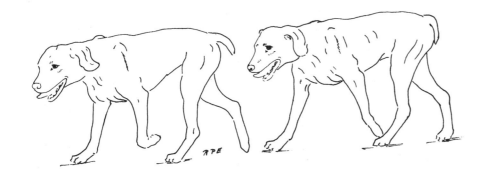

Care must be taken to distinguish faulty "loose" shoulders with too much play at the withers from the muscular flexible shoulders normal for breeds having occupational requirements that permit the body to drop between the shoulders in trailing or crouching. Hounds and spaniels may exhibit such working posture, and anyone who has watched herding dogs creeping alertly behind restless livestock, ready to turn in a flash to control breakaways, can appreciate the need for front-end flexibility as a useful and even life-saving tool.

Chapter 8

Heads and Tails...

And a Few Other Views

A willing worker is a pleasure to watch.

Semantics and Optical Illusion Can Cause Confusion in Understanding Gait

A few terms cause considerable misunderstanding about front and rear action, simply because they are used without clear definition. Expressions such as *parallel, standing straight, moving straight, inclining inward, moving close, toeing in, moving on the same plane, parallel tracks, parallel hocks, single tracking* and others, not only confuse newcomers, but now and then cause lively discussion among some who have been in the dog game for many years.

The unfortunate aspect of this problem of semantics is that it occasionally permits one to condone certain faulty action, or casts a shadow on action that is correct. It is also a possible reason for faults being perpetuated by innocent parties who try to breed dogs to move in a way never intended by nature. There is a common fallacy, for example, that trotting dogs should move with their legs parallel with each other. Surely such thinking must be influenced by optical illusion, for slow motion photography has long since shown that normal leg movement inclines slightly inward, dependent—of course— on the type of dog and his rate of travel. Misunderstanding of this principle has brought the unjust criticism of "moving too close" on many a dog that actually is moving well. Parallel movement is contrary to nature's laws of balance and motion. Breeders who try to achieve it must sacrifice angulation, and handlers who try to achieve it must resort to tight leads, substituting stilted short action for good natural reach.

The sequence sketches that follow illustrate variations in gaiting as dogs come and go from the viewer, and should help to clarify more of the common faults that often puzzle us.

The Normal Stance

"Parallel" and "Standing Straight"

A dog of good stature stands naturally with his weight evenly distributed at the four corners of his body. Seen from the rear, the legs appear to stand parallel to each other and reasonably straight from hip through stifle and hock to pads.

The column of support from shoulder joint through elbow and carpals to pads is also reasonably straight. The natural tendency of the toes to stand just off the vertical line is for balance, much as a human stands with his feet turned slightly outward, or as a sprinter—just before take-off—rests in a forward position with his fingers on the ground.

In this standing position the dog's legs are parallel, and may seem to appear parallel as he starts to walk because, at the walk, the body is supported by three legs with each step and there is little problem with balance. However, as the dog moves faster there is a natural tendency for the limbs to reach inward, called "convergence" or "the tendency to single track." How and why a dog does this is discussed in the following pages.

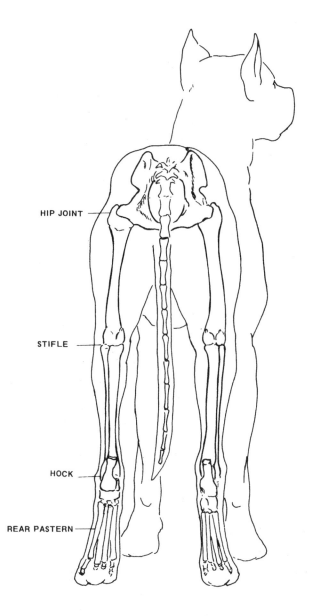

HIP JOINT

STIFLE

HOCK

REAR PASTERN

91

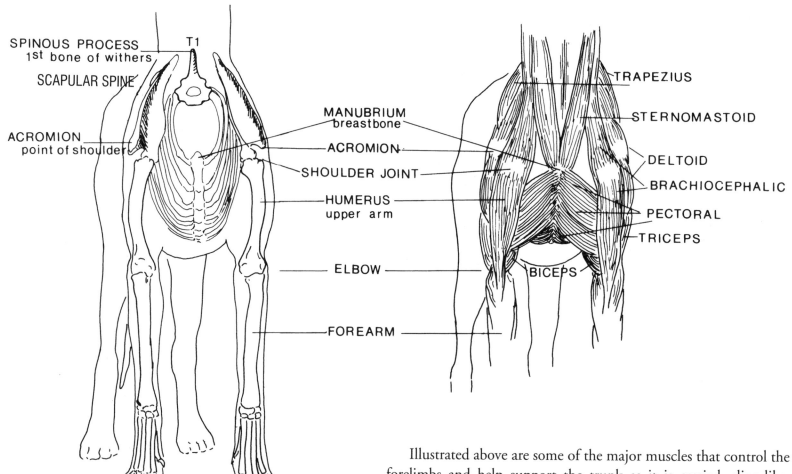

SPINOUS PROCESS
1st bone of withers
T1

SCAPULAR SPINE

ACROMION
point of shoulder

MANUBRIUM
breastbone

ACROMION

SHOULDER JOINT

HUMERUS
upper arm

ELBOW

FOREARM

TRAPEZIUS

STERNOMASTOID

DELTOID

BRACHIOCEPHALIC

PECTORAL

TRICEPS

BICEPS

Because of the contour of the forechest, where the ribs are quite flat, *the shoulder blades set at an angle that is oblique—not parallel—to the spine.* The forward edges are deeply embedded in muscle, thus difficult to feel, and for this reason are often confused with the scapular spines. This oblique position has a direct bearing on limb movement because as the blades glide over the ribs the lift and swing is slightly inward.

Illustrated above are some of the major muscles that control the forelimbs and help support the trunk as it is carried, sling-like, within the pectoral girdle (front assembly). As previously mentioned, the dog has no collarbone to serve as a stabilizing buttress or strut between the lower blades and the breastbone. This places considerable stress on the muscles and gives rise to thick bones at the shoulder joint and noticeable prominence to the acromion (point of shoulder) which projects outward from the lower end of the scapular spine. The muscles sketched in the above diagram are an important factor in lifting, extending and retracting the forelimbs, as well as in controlling body balance as the dog's speed increases.

The Physical Reasons for Limb Convergence Toward a Center Line of Travel

To more clearly understand the principle of convergence—or how a dog tries to maintain balance over a center line of travel—it is important to visualize the shape of the forechest and how the shoulder assembly is positioned against it. In all dogs the ribcages are oval in shape, but some are rounder than others, some slimmer, some deeper, some shallower, some longer, and some shorter. Whatever the differences, there is in each dog a gradual narrowing of the chest wall where the first few ribs gradually become flatter and shorter as the sternum inclines upward toward the manubrium. This creates a smooth surface for the blades to lie at an oblique, not parallel, position along the contour of the forechest, setting the stage for the inward swing of the forelimbs.

Coordinating with the fore and aft swing of the scapula, the humerus (upper arm) moves freely along the lower chest wall (sternum)—see pages 75-79. Due to the ball and socket nature of the scapula-humeral joint, the humerus is able to absorb transversal movement with the hinge-like conformation of the elbow joint. Along with the action of the triceps muscle the humerus thus controls the in and out flexion of the elbow.

Equally important in the overall picture is how the rear limbs move in coordination with the front. In the hindquarters the play of the muscle group on the hip sockets—also of ball and socket design—lends flexibility to the femurs in moving wide to avoid interference with the posterior aspect of the ribcage during the gallop. In any of the joints, front or rear, irregularities in articulation, bone deformities, or poor muscular control, impair efficient movement. The degree of convergence depends on the kind of dog and the speed at which it is moving.

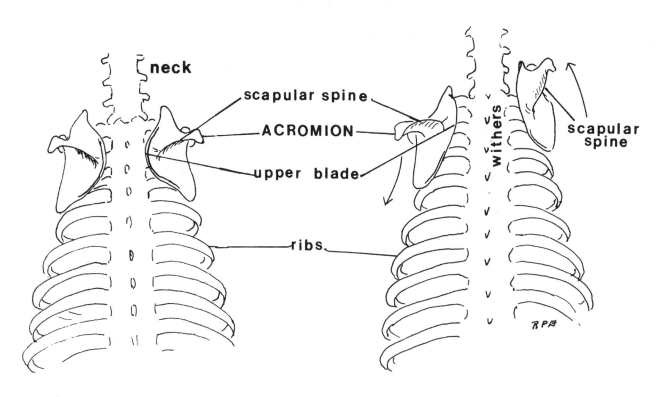

neck

scapular spine

ACROMION

upper blade

ribs

withers

scapular spine

Cineradiography reveals the position of the shoulder blades as one looks down on the dog's back, on the left as the dog stands, on the right as he moves. The placement of the blades follows the description detailed on the opposite page. The upper tips are what we feel when we run our hands over the lower neckline, sending an important message about slant of the blades, width of the forechest, and muscular and physical condition. It is not a question of "the closer the tips the better," because it is possible for a narrow chest combined with steeply set shoulders to create a pinching effect that may hamper free movement, particularly as the dog lowers his head in retrieving, trailing and even eating. The right diagram shows the blades as they glide over the forward portion of the chest wall toward a center line of balance.

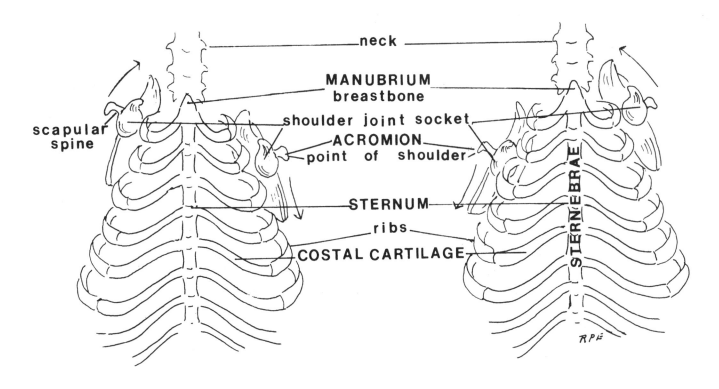

neck

MANUBRIUM
breastbone

scapular
spine

shoulder joint socket

ACROMION
point of shoulder

STERNUM

ribs

COSTAL CARTILAGE

STERNEBRAE

RPF

The diagrams above are taken from cineradiographic studies (moving X-rays) showing the ribcage *beneath* a fox terrier. While the blades may resemble "flying saucers" these illustrations show how the bones glide back and forth along the narrowing contour of the forechest, with the forward edges facing inward. For the sake of clarity, the upper arms (humerus) and legs are not included—thus, only the shoulder joint sockets, acromia and insides of the blades are visible. A lateral view shows the scapular spines as prominent ridges that run from the acromia up the center of the blades, which is what one usually feels for in evaluating shoulder layback. The scapular spines provide anchorage for heavy muscling required to stabilize and control movement of the blades. (See page 47)

Normal Leg Position at the Trot "Moving Straight"

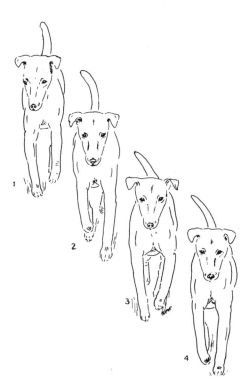

When a dog breaks into a trot, his body is supported by only two legs at a time, which move as alternating diagonal pairs. He must therefore balance himself, as nearly as possible, over a center column of support, in order to travel easily and efficiently; otherwise he will sway from side to side. To achieve balance, his legs angle inward toward a center line beneath his body, and the greater the speed, the closer they come to tracking on a straight line, much as a human runs with one foot in front of the other to keep his body from rocking. Variations in the dog's height, breadth of body and length of leg, influence the extent to which the legs incline inward, but all dogs make the effort—regardless of breed or type.

The angle of inclination begins with the shoulders and hips, and in the majority of breeds the limbs should remain relatively straight, even as they flex or extend. Such action is described as "moving straight." Flexion in the carpal joints keeps the swing legs from interfering with the supporting legs. The natural law of balance is one of the most important factors in understanding gait as dogs come and go from the viewer. Normal convergence should never be confused with the fault of "moving close."

Single Tracking: Many dogs single track as they move faster, leaving footprints that fall on or close to a center line.

Parallel Tracking: Others leave parallel tracks, where the footprints fall wider apart on either side of the center line of travel. Speed and build influence the degree to which the limbs converge.

The criteria of judgment is not whether a dog single tracks, or whether he has a wider footfall; it is **how** and **why** he moves as he does that must be understood and evaluated against overall conformation and the purpose for which the breed was developed. Regardless of differences, the principle of seeking balanced support remains the same for all, as this is Nature's way of offsetting wasteful action that reduces efficiency.

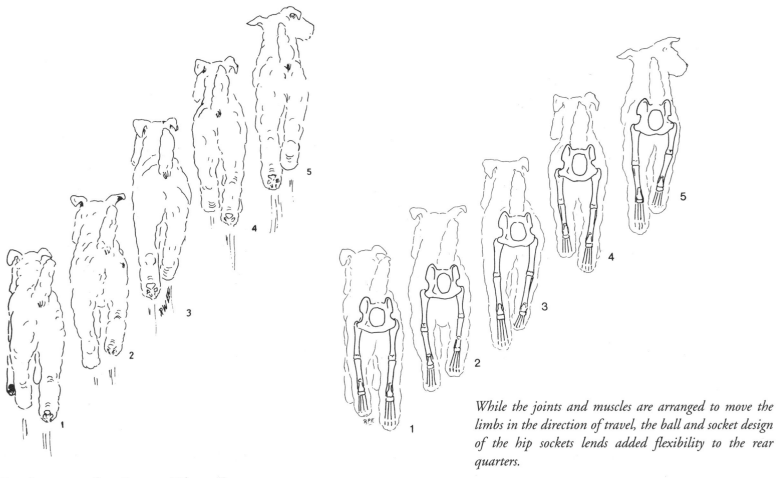

While the joints and muscles are arranged to move the limbs in the direction of travel, the ball and socket design of the hip sockets lends added flexibility to the rear quarters.

Legs "Moving on the Same Plane"

Each leg should move in line with the leg ahead of, or behind it, inclining no more and no less. Viewed directly from the rear, the hind legs should tend to cover the plane of the front, and vice versa. There should be no twisting of the joints other than the normal flexibility provided by nature for the passing legs to avoid interference with the legs that are in support. But there are a few exceptions—see next page.

"Rolling"

A few breeds, such as the Bulldog or Pekingese, are normally broader in the front quarters than they are in the rear. This type of conformation causes the hind feet to track within the footfall of the front. The wide diagonal thrust contributes to a characteristic, almost swaggering or rolling action, but this should not be exaggerated.

Legs "Not Moving on the Same Plane" (fault)

When the hind feet do not follow the tracks made by the front feet, the legs are not inclining inward to the same extent and action is faulty. Many gaiting faults fall under this category. But again, there are exceptions—see the facing page.

Front feet moving wide, hind feet moving on center line.

Hind feet moving wide, front feet moving on center line.

Moving wide in front and tracking on a single line in the rear. In this illustration the left hock tends to twist as it bears weight.

Tracking too wide behind. This type of action may be caused by tight ligaments, or may indicate trouble in the stifle joints.

"Crabbing" (fault)

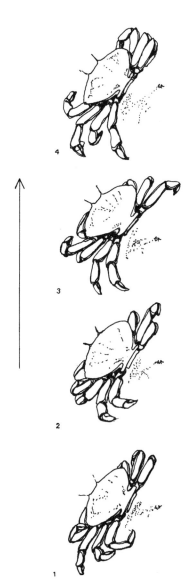

"Crabbing" is a common fault in which the dog moves with his body at an angle to the line of travel. The action is frequently due to more angulation in the rear than in the front, in combination with a short, stiff back.

When a dog takes longer steps with his hind legs than with his forelimbs, he can avoid striking or interfering by trotting with hindquarters swung to one side. However, because the legs do not "move on the same plane," the gait is awkward and inefficient.

Crabbing may also indicate spinal injury, as the dog twists to relieve strain. Occasionally, it is the result of habit from constant heeling and watching the owner.

The term "crabbing" originates with the sea crab, which crawls forward in sidewise fashion. The fault is also occasionally referred to as "yawing," or as "side-winding." Careless handling or lack of leash training often causes dogs that normally would move straight to "crab."

"Crabbing" and "Crossing in the Rear" (faults)

Roached Back with "Crabbing" (faults)

Below:
A roached back is a stiff back, often seen with crabbing or pacing. This particular dog is taller than he is long, giving him proportions that accentuate the problem of trying to avoid leg interference. A roached back is often the result of strain or spinal disorder.

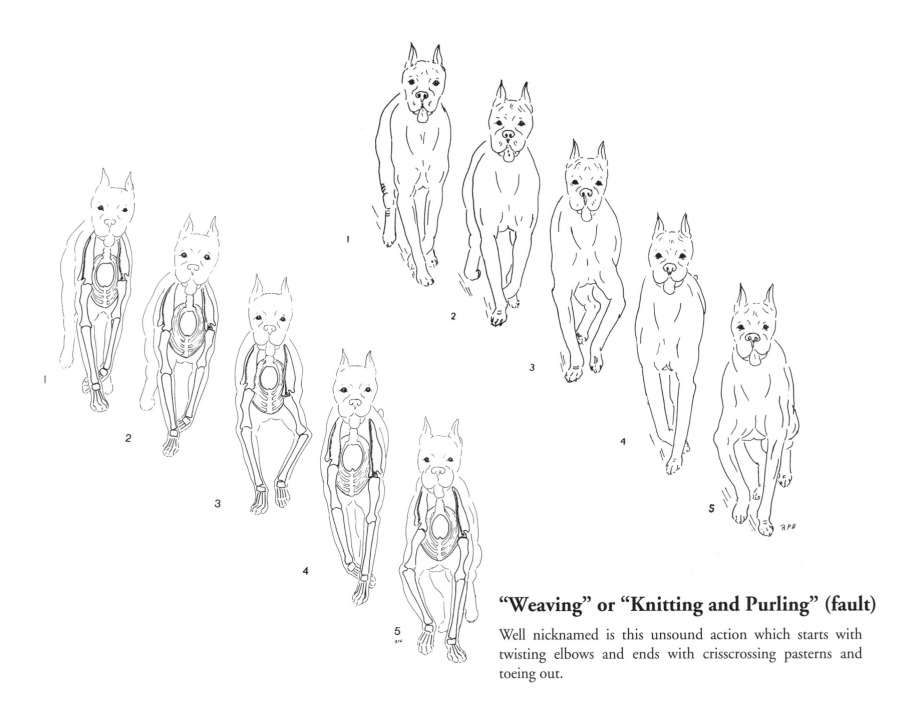

"Weaving" or "Knitting and Purling" (fault)

Well nicknamed is this unsound action which starts with twisting elbows and ends with crisscrossing pasterns and toeing out.

"Moving Close" and "Stifles Out" (faults)

When the hocks turn in, and the pasterns drop straight to the ground and move parallel to one another, the dog is "moving close" in the rear. In some cases, as in this illustration, the stifle is also thrown out of line. Action of this sort places severe strain on ligaments and muscles.

"Moving Close" and "Brushing" (faults)

Top: Parallel pasterns are sometimes so close that the legs "brush" in passing
Below: Interfering and Crossing (*faults*)

"Cowhocks" (fault)

Cows often stand with their hocks turned in and their stifles turned out to accommodate large udders more comfortably. "Cowhocks" in dogs seriously weaken rear thrust.

This dog is not only cowhocked, but is also crossing his legs in front—a fault no doubt accentuated because he is pulling away from his handler.

Patella Luxation

"Snatching Hocks" (fault)—a symptom of stifle trouble. This structural defect is indicated by a quick outward or inward snatching of the hocks, or sometimes a skipping action, as the rear legs twist in beneath the body. It is a compensation for discomfort in the stifle joints where the patellas (kneecaps) slip out of the trochlear grooves at the base of the femurs (thigh bones). The problem causes noticeable rocking in the rear quarters. The subject of the above series illustrates a known case of bilateral patella luxation.

"Spread Hocks" (fault)

Hocks that turn out are called "spread hocks," "barrel hocks," or "hocking out." Like other faults, it shows up in varying degrees of severity. It always causes the feet to "toe in" (just the opposite from "cowhocks," which causes "toeing out").

"Spread hocks," combined with "crossing in front."

"Twisting Hocks" (fault)

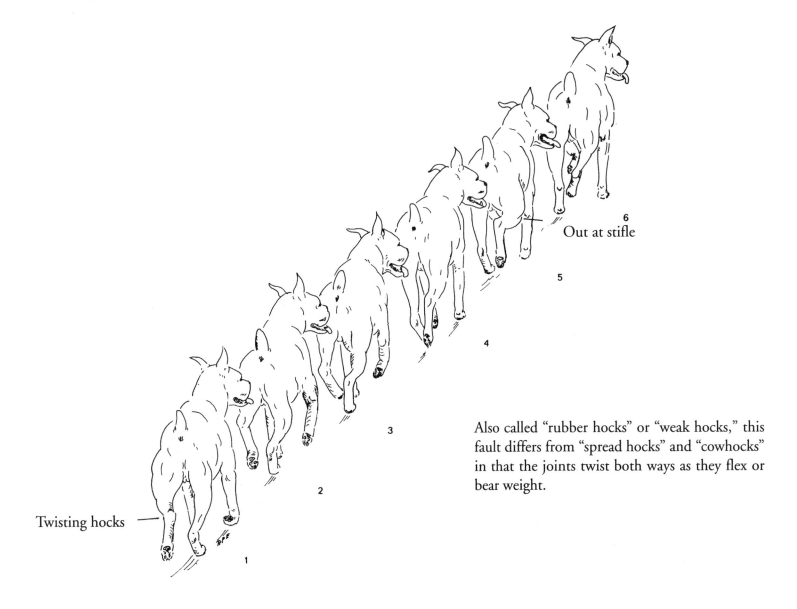

Twisting hocks

6
Out at stifle

5

4

3

2

1

Also called "rubber hocks" or "weak hocks," this fault differs from "spread hocks" and "cowhocks" in that the joints twist both ways as they flex or bear weight.

"Pitching" and "Crossing" (faults)

"Pitching" is characterized by severe rocking of the haunches as the rear legs swing forward in a wide arc rather than flexing and driving through the stifle and hock. Sway of the body may be so pronounced that at times both front and rear feet cross the center line. Croup problems may also be linked to faulty fronts, twisting in the central body, spread hocks or severe cowhocks.

*Twisting joints mean wear and tear on ligaments—more than
sufficient reason for complete exhaustion after a day in the field.*

"Pitching" combined with "Cowhocks" (faults)

Because of their structure, short-legged, broadly-built dogs move with some body roll, but those that move well minimize this tendency through the natural inclination of the legs toward a center line of balance beneath their bodies.

Left: Moving well in front, but "toeing-out" in the rear ("cowhocks")

Right: Good rear movement.

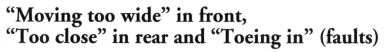

**"Moving too wide" in front,
"Too close" in rear and "Toeing in" (faults)**

**"Toeing Out" or the
"East-West Front" (fault)**

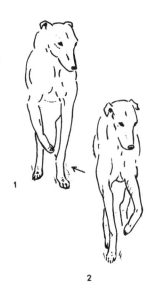

Arrows point to weak carpal joints, which bend inward, causing the feet to turn out.

114

Championship Titles Do Not Guarantee Perfection

If you plan to raise dogs, study the pedigrees carefully. Most faults tend to be inherited, and serious defects which become deeply entrenched can imperil the soundness of breeding programs.

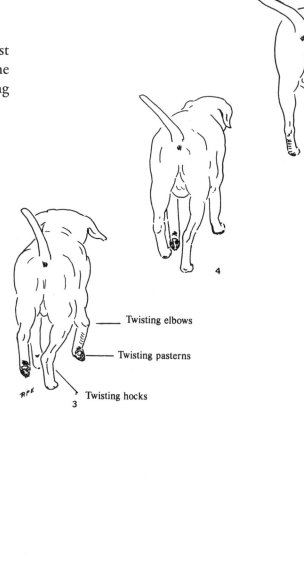

5   Toeing in

4

Twisting elbows

Twisting pasterns

Twisting hocks

3

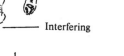

Interfering

2

1

Out at the Elbows (fault)

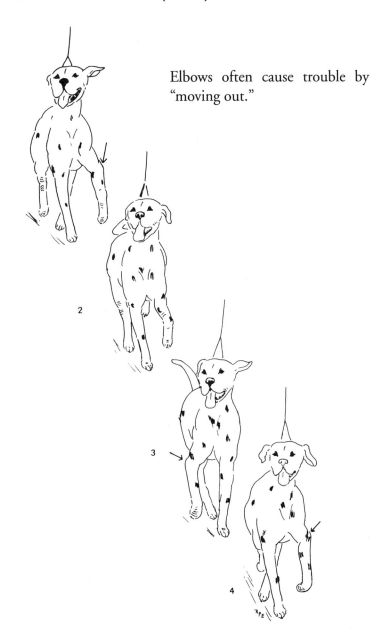

Elbows often cause trouble by "moving out."

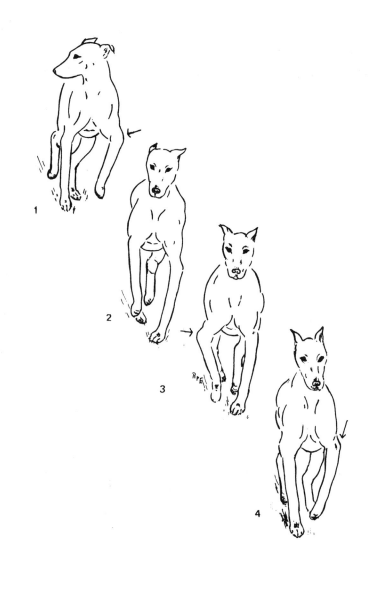

116

"Tied at the Elbows" or "Paddling" (fault)

This is just the opposite sort of action from elbows moving out, and is generally considered a more serious defect because it so severely restricts front movement. Pinching in at the elbows, as well as the shoulder joints, causes the front legs to swing forward on a stiff outward arc. Because of the wide footfall, the dog is said to travel "basewide," and the body rocks from side to side.

The term "paddling" derives from the swing and dip of the paddle as the canoeist keeps his canoe on course.

117

A Few Hints on Handling

If we plan to exhibit in dogs shows, we should give our dogs the advantage they deserve through careful handling. Good handling brings out the best in a dog. Poor handling can impair his overall appearance, and give the impression of faults that are not really there.

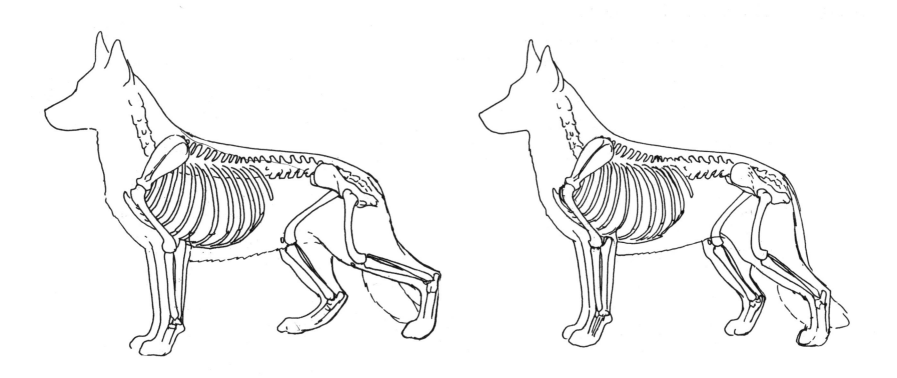

Dogs are often posed in show stance to accentuate bend of stifle and hock, a position that drops the topline and changes the angle of the pelvic assembly. Excessive angulation, even temporary, can weaken joint support—shown in the dog on the left.

A Tight Lead is Often Detrimental

The inexperienced handler may create the appearance of faulty gaiting by restricting the dog's natural (and proper) movement. Conversely, a handler may try to hide gaiting flaws by suspending the dog under the lead.

Swinging from the end of a tight lead causes this dog to "cross" in front.

Side pull on the lead accentuates the dog's tendency to "cross."

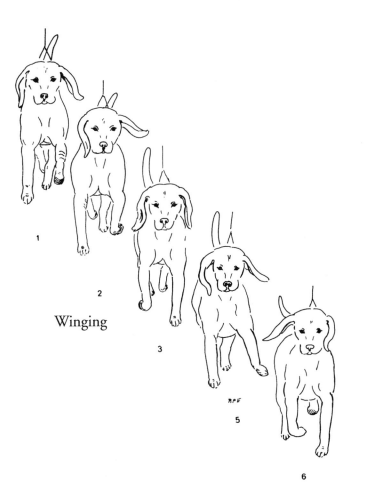

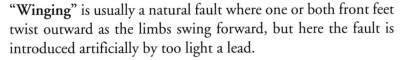

Winging

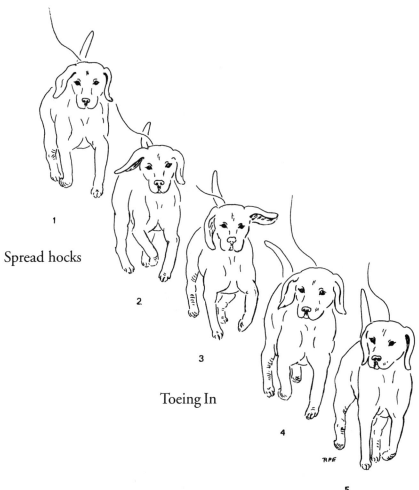

Spread hocks

Toeing In

"**Winging**" is usually a natural fault where one or both front feet twist outward as the limbs swing forward, but here the fault is introduced artificially by too light a lead.

At the judge's request, "Loose lead, please," the same dog trots freely and exhibits his natural inclination to "**move wide in the hocks**," "**out at the elbows**," and "**toe in**," all of which are gaiting flaws.

When the judge requests that you "gait your dog" in the show ring, the straight-on approach is important—but remember, it is the dog, not you, who is under judgment.

Breeding programs based on sound structure and stable temperament lay the foundation for close partnerships, with willingness to meet the task at hand, whatever the call.

Conclusion

At risk of being considered a "fault finder," the author may appear to have dwelt rather heavily on what makes a dog move incorrectly—and not have stressed enough the features that make him move well. Unfortunately, faults tend to linger in one's impression, and too often override the total perspective. Such an imbalance was not our intent, but if our emphasis has stirred awareness of a few structural pitfalls that threaten the quality of many present day breeds, then it will have served a useful purpose.

Although you might find it difficult to put into words what you are looking for in good movement, you may have sensed it without knowing why. It may be just the feeling of pleasure over the flashy gait of a stylish entry in the show ring, or the thrill of excitement that comes with watching a hunting dog work smoothly across a field and suddenly freeze on point. You may instinctively have sensed the importance of stamina if you have hunted over a retriever that swims strongly and eagerly at the close of a strenuous day in the marshes. Or, if you are one who has handled a willing dog through obedience or agility competition, where advanced training demands constant effort in jumping, you have experienced the need for soundness.

Too often puppies are selected solely on the basis of their expression, personality, color, coat texture or size-traits, which, to be sure, give each its special appeal and add to the joy of the owner. But these traits alone are not enough. Structure must also be considered if a breed or strain is to be kept strong. So it is to the breeders who know what to look for and what to avoid, who know what makes a good dog move well and why, that novices should turn for guidance and learning. Experience is a good teacher, but knowledge—with a little luck!—steers the shortest way to lasting success.

References—and books of interest

Bracket, Lyoyd C. and Horswell, Laurence A., "The Dog in Motion," *Dog World Magazine* (USA) August 1961-October 1965.

Brown, Curtis and Thelma, *Art and Science of Judging Dogs*, B&E Publications, Inc., Hollywood, CA.

The Canine, *A Veterinary Aid in Anatomical Transparencie*s, Fromm Laboratories, Inc. Grafton, Wisconsin, 1967.

Ellenberger, Baum, and Dittrich, *An Atlas of Animal Anatomy for Artists*, Dover Publications, Inc., New York, 1967.

Gardiner, Catherine, *Dogs—As a Hobby or Profession*, Vol. 1, 11, Canine Consultants, Ltd., Ontario, Canada

Gilbert, Edward M., Jr., & Brown, Thelma R., *Structure and Terminology*, Howell Book House, NY, 1995

Hollenbeck, Leon, *The Dynamics of Canine Gait*, Hollenbeck, NY, 1971.

Horner, Tom, *Take Them Around Please*, Douglas David & Charles, Ltd., Canada, 1975

Hourdebaigt, Jean-Pierre and Seymour, Shari L., *Canine Massage*, Howell Book House, NY, 1999.

Jenkins, Farish A., Jr., *The Movement of the Shoulder in the Claviculate and Aclaviculate Mammals*, Department of Biology, Museum of Comparative Zoology, Harvard University, Cambridge, MA.

Lyon, McDowell, *The Dog in Action*, Howell Book House, NY, 1950.

Miller, Christensen and Evans, *Anatomy of the Dog*, W. B. Saunders, Philadelphia, London, 1964.

Miller, Constance O., *Gazehounds, The Search for Truth*, Hoflin Publishing Ltd., Wheat Ridge, CO, 1988.

Smythe, R. H., *The Anatomy of Dog Breeding*, Popular Dogs Publishing Co., London, 1962.

Smythe, R. H., *Dog Structure and Movement*, Popular Dogs Publishing Co., London, 1970.

Smythe, R. H., *The Conformation of the Dog*, Popular Dogs Publishing Co., London, 1957.

Spira, Harry R., *Canine Terminology*, Harper & Rowe, Publishers, Sydney, 1982.

Stillman, J. D. B., *The Horse in Motion*, James Osgood & Co., Boston, 1882.

"Stonehenge", *The Dogs of the British Islands*, 2nd edition, London, 1872.

Wynmalen, Henry, *The Horse in Action*, 2nd printing, Jarrod & Sons, Ltd., Norwich, England, 1956.

Zink, M. Christine & Daniels, Julie, *Jumping From A to Z*, Canine Sport Productions, Lutherville, MD, 1995.

Index